[the NUMBER #1 ONE SECRETS OF successful MANAGERS

Everything You Need to Know About Managing Others

HAL PITT

POWER POTENTIALS

the NUMBER ONE SECRETS OF successful MANAGERS

The Number One Secrets of Successful Managers
© March 2003 Power Potentials Publishing

    Power Potentials Publishing
    P.O. Box 184
    Cascade CO 80809

Cover Design by Angie Durbin
Book Layout by Bill Groetzinger

The Number One Secrets of Successful Managers
LCCN #2002108822
ISBN #0-971-4437-4-2

CONTENTS

The Number One Secrets of Successful Managers

ACKNOWLEDGEMENTS

Writing a book is never an individual effort. It takes the beliefs and talents of others to make good things happen. I would like to thank the following individuals for making my dream of authoring a book come true:

To Meryl Runion, my publisher. Your belief in my book and commitment to taking on an unknown and unproven author will always keep me wondering, "Why me?"

To Milli Thornton and Kristin Porotsky, my editors. Thank you for showing me how poor a writer I am by turning my words and phrases to gold.

To Angie Durbin, my graphics artist. The way you turned my inept cover design suggestions into something that far surpasses my talent and imagination will always fill me with awe.

To Mark Sanborn, Brian Tracey, Linda Larsen, Scott McKain, and Jay Conrad Levinson, my endorsers. Thank you for reading my book and putting your reputations on the line for a man you don't even know.

And, most important of all...

To Nancy, my honey of a wife whose twenty-six years of commitment to a lunatic makes me the luckiest man on the face of the planet.

The Number One Secrets of Successful Managers

Did you know:

- 85% of those in management positions have never had management training. *—1999 Harris Poll*
- 80% of the problems in organizations today are due to structural or functional inadequacies due to ineffective management.

What do the above statistics have in common? If you thought, "Poor management," you'd be right. Most organizational difficulties aren't caused by poor employee performance and attitudes, but by managers who don't know how to manage their people properly.

> *"Sustainable company excellence comes from a huge stable of able managers. Great managers are an organization's glue."*
>
> —TOM PETERS

How are you doing as a manager right now? Are you confident in your abilities—or are you having problems getting your employees to do the jobs they were hired to do? Are you barely treading water in your efforts to motivate your employees toward excellence? Are you having problems gaining employee commitment to the mission and vision of the organization? Are your employees getting burned out because they are continually being asked to do more for less? If so, help is just the flip of a page away.

This book is for those who want to perform well as a manager or supervisor. It's for those who want to join the ranks of managers who know how to get the best from their employees. Within these pages you will learn what many great managers have learned and put into practice. The information contained in this book isn't as much a result of what the "experts" in management and leadership are saying, as what thousands of managers and supervisors around the country like you have told me works in practice, not just theory. Some of the information in this book comes from the wisdom of our grandmothers and grandfathers, and the "old hats" that have been managing effectively for decades.

If you are a new manager, get ready for a great ride. If you're a seasoned manager, ask yourself if you are practicing the concepts and skills outlined in this book. If your answer is no, challenge yourself to do so.

Your employees deserve a manager who knows how to manage effectively. YOU ARE THE GLUE! Your boss is counting on you to get maximum performance from each of your employees.

NOW IT'S TIME TO LEARN HOW!

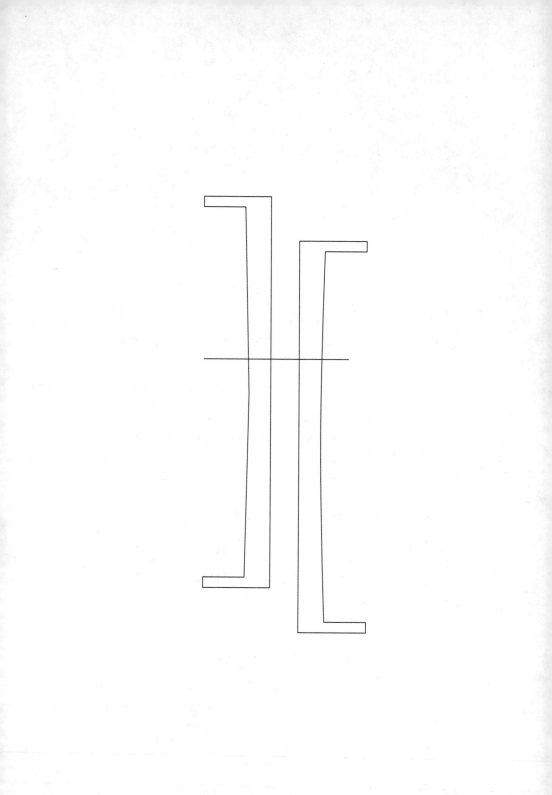

CHAPTER 1

The #1 Job of Every Manager

When you walk into your office or cubicle every day as a manager or supervisor, do you know what your #1 job is?

- Is it to motivate your employees?

- Is it to listen?

- Is it to be a mentor and a coach?

Your organization is paying you to accomplish something, and you need to know what that something is. Your CEO is counting on you to do this every day.

Do you know what your #1 job as a manager or supervisor is?

TURN THE PAGE TO FIND OUT! ☞

The Number One Secrets of Successful Managers

Your #1 Job as a Manager Is to...

Make Sure Your Employees Are Doing the Jobs They Were Hired To Do

That's it! That's why you're getting paid more than your employees. *(If you are not paid more, ask for the raise that's due you.)* Your job is to get maximum performance from each of your workers.

What Successful Organizations Know

Most organizations in the world are about this: An organization either has a quality product, a quality service, or both, that it wants to provide to the consumer. The organization hopes the consumer will buy the product or use the service so it will continue to make money—the bottom line. Your job as a manager is to make sure your employees are providing that quality product or service to the consumer, so that your company makes money.

What does Southwest Airlines want to provide? Of course, it wants to provide quality flying at affordable prices. What is the CEO counting on? He's counting on his managers to ensure employees are providing quality service.

What does Wendy's restaurant want to provide? We all know they want to provide their customers with the best tasting hamburgers on the planet. What is the CEO counting on? He's counting on his managers to ensure that employees are providing quality food and services.

Think about it. If you were the CEO of your company, wouldn't you be counting on your managers to get maximum performance from each employee? And, as the CEO, if a quality product or service is not being provided, whom do you go to? The employee? Of course not! You'll go to the manager of that department to find out why the employee isn't providing the quality product or service that is the life-blood of the company.

Two Lessons Successful Managers Have Learned

Here are two important lessons that must be learned right away if you're going to get the best performance from your employees:

Lesson #1:

MANAGERS ARE NOT HIRED TO BE ANYONE'S FRIEND, BUT, RATHER, ARE HIRED TO BE FRIENDLY!

Your job is to make sure your employees are doing their jobs. Do not fall into the trap of thinking everyone should like you as a manager. It isn't realistic. Not everyone will like you, and that's just fine. If you're friendly, respectful, kind, and fair to all your employees equally, most of them will have great respect for you. But no matter how friendly and fair you are to all employees, there is bound to be one employee who doesn't like you and will never like you. If that employee wants to go home and speak poorly of you to family and friends, don't fret about it. BUT AT WORK, EVERY MANAGER AND EMPLOYEE MUST BE REQUIRED TO PUT FORTH A PROFESSIONAL ATTITUDE AND DO THE JOB HE OR SHE WAS HIRED TO DO! Anything less should not be tolerated. It is management's responsibility to create an environment conducive to peak performance and behavior. It's the employee's responsibility to perform quality work and behave professionally in that environment.

Lesson #2:

MANAGERS MUST DRAW THE LINE ON SOCIAL RELATIONSHIPS WITH THOSE THEY MANAGE AT WORK.

Once you are promoted to a supervisory or management position, you must draw the line on social relationships with those who were previously your peers. You cannot gather around the water cooler or go out to lunch with them like you used to. You cannot have your friends in your office talking about the latest movie or sports event like you used to. If you do go out to lunch with them once in a while, YOU MUST invite other employees also. If you are going to the movies, invite other employees. Tell your friends that you must draw the line on your social relationships at work and that you can't "hang out" with them like you used to.

The reason for this is simple. If you continue to behave with your close friends as usual, in a very short time your other employees will start saying one of the most dangerous words that can be said of any manager: FAVORITISM. Let all employees know you desire a trusting and professional working relationship. Get one-on-one with your friends and ask for their understanding on this new paradigm—that at work you must keep your relationships professional. If they are your friends, they will respect your feelings and work hard for you. If not, they weren't truly your friends in the first place.

The Price Managers Pay

Management is a lonely place at times. It requires energy and passion to do it right. Managers must be willing to be unpopular sometimes, make waves, and possibly lose a friend here and there. Effective management comes with a price.

It is essential that you are clear in what your management priorities are. It is not to be liked by everyone, and it's not to be everyone's friend. Your #1 priority, your #1 job as a manager, is to ensure that your employees are doing the jobs they were hired to do. Your CEO is counting on you to get quality performance and behavior from each of your employees. And if that means making decisions that are sometimes unpopular to maintain the bottom line, so be it.

Learning to Manage Effectively

In this chapter, you have discovered that the #1 job of a manager is to make sure employees are doing the jobs they were hired to do. The rest of the book is about learning how to do it right.

Action Plan

Are Your Employees Doing the Jobs They Were Hired To Do?

On a piece of paper, write down the names of the employees you directly manage. Rate each employee on a scale of 1–5 (5 being the best) in terms of performance and behavior.

Name	*Performance*	*Behavior*
_____	1 2 3 4 5	1 2 3 4 5

Did you rate any of your employees a 1 or 2 in performance? If so, that means they may not be providing your customers with a quality product or service. Did you rate any of your employees a 1 or 2 in behavior? If so, they may be hurting customer service, and the morale and team spirit in your department.

Next to the employee(s) that you rated low in either performance or behavior, write down the difficulty you are having and what you are doing to rectify the issue.

Name of Employee: _____

Difficulty You're Experiencing:

_____

_____

_____

_____

What You are Doing About It:

_____

_____

As a manager, you are held accountable for an employee's low performance and/or behavior in that department. You must deal with the problem in a timely manner.

If you do not know how to get quality performance or behavior from your substandard employee(s), don't let that concern you at this point. For now, just be aware of the performance and behavioral issues of each of your employees. Awareness is the beginning of your successful journey as a manager. The strategies that you can use to get peak performance and behaviors come next.

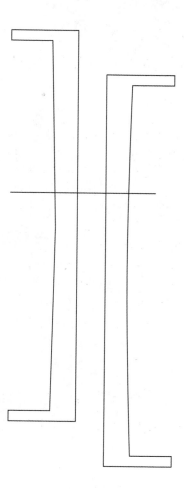

CHAPTER 2

The #1 Purpose of Every Organization

Your organization exists for a reason. There is a reason the founder of your company endured great pains and sleepless nights to make things happen. Whether it's General Motors or a mom and pop ice cream store, the men and women at the top who give the orders want something to happen on a daily basis. If this #1 purpose isn't reached, the bottom line will suffer and a "Going Out of Business" sign will ultimately be hung on the door.

You've learned that your #1 goal as a manager is to ensure your employees are doing the jobs they were hired to do. By ensuring a quality product or service, you will help your organization reach its #1 purpose every day. Understanding the #1 purpose of your organization will help you see the big picture, and realize just how important it is that you are fulfilling your duties as a manager.

What is the #1 Purpose of Every Organization?

TURN THE PAGE TO FIND OUT! ☞

The #1 Purpose of Every Organization Is to...

Create and Retain Customers

"The purpose of business is to create and retain customers."

—PETER DRUCKER

Create and Retain Customers

For an organization to remain successful and make money in today's competitive economy, it must—through sleek advertising, marketing, and quality products and services—create and retain customers. This is why you must understand the importance of your job as a manager. By tolerating poor performance and behavior, you run the risk of destroying an organization. Yes, destroying. The history of business is fraught with examples of companies going bankrupt, losing customers, or enduring million dollar lawsuits due to one or more of its employees not providing a quality product or service.

Why Quality Customer Service Is a Must

Managers must demand that their employees meet company standards of performance and behavior. Through coaching, counseling, discipline, and creating an environment conducive to excellence, managers must require that employees do the jobs they were hired to do. The following statistics on customer service show us why:

- **68% of customers go elsewhere because the people they dealt with were indifferent to their needs.**
- **The average unhappy customer will share the negative experience with 9 other people.**
- **The average unhappy customer will remember the incident for 23-1/2 years.**
- **The average happy customer will talk about the pleasant experience for 18 months.**
- **91% of dissatisfied customers do not complain, but will never buy from the business again.**
- **83% of sales are based on the customer liking the salesperson.**

According to statistics compiled by the White House Office of Customer Affairs

The Best Organization "Delights" Its Customers

These statistics show us that businesses can no longer merely satisfy the customer. In fact, the old adage, "customer satisfaction," is dead. To be competitive today and create and retain customers, companies must now delight the customer. Organizations must go above and beyond "satisfactory," and provide customers with products and services that are superior. Customers look for the best, or something a little different, and are not satisfied with the mundane and mediocre anymore.

Taco Bell is a prime example of customer delight. It is constantly coming out with "new and improved" products. Through effective advertising and marketing, the company lures us in to try their new tacos or burritos.

Doubletree Inn knows the importance of delighting its patrons. After check in, they hand you a huge chocolate chip cookie. I know business travelers who prefer to stay at Doubletree Inn because of the cookies.

And what does each of these companies expect of its managers? To ensure their employees are delighting customers through quality products and services. An employee who continues to exert minimal effort and is abrasive toward other employees and/or customers cannot be allowed to remain in an organization.

Delighting External Customers

Our external customers—those who come to our business every day—want to feel welcomed, understood, and important. They want to feel comforted when they have issues with our products and services. The best organizations have core values that stress the importance of delighting customers on a daily basis, demanding that their employees live according to those values. The best organizations teach their employees exactly what exceptional customer service is, and empower them to meet the customer's expectations. They teach employees service phrases, such as, "How can I help you?" and "I don't know the answer, but I'll get it for you." The best companies do everything within their power to exceed customer expectations.

Managers must instruct their employees on the #1 purpose of the organization. Employees must know they are the foundation of the organization; that their performance and behavior can make or break its overall success. Employees are ambassadors, and they must be given the tools to delight customers. Employees must also be held accountable for quality performance and behavior.

Delighting Internal Customers

Much is written and said about delighting the external customer, but what of the internal customer? Every person we work with is a customer. Departments provide resources to other departments; employees provide resources and services to each other. Just as high standards of performance and conduct are demanded for our external customers, so should organizations demand high standards of performance and conduct internally.

Every employee must be treated with dignity and respect. *Why?* So management can create and retain its best employees. Every employee should be given the opportunity to grow and succeed. *Why?* So management can create and retain its best employees. The best organizations don't treat their employees like numbers, but like the valued members that they are.

As managers, we should be going out of our way to "delight" our employees. Rewards, benefits, small tokens of appreciation, a kind word, and spending extra time to help an employee succeed are just a few examples of what we can do on an ongoing basis to create a delightful climate at work. Through our good examples, we will show employees how important it is that they do what they can to delight their fellow team members.

Make sure your employees are provided training on how to delight both internal and external customers. Hold them accountable for their performance and behavior. By doing so, your organization will continue to make money and fulfill its #1 purpose—which is to create and retain customers.

Action Plan

Are You "Delighting" Your Customers?

On a piece of paper, write down three things your organization is doing to exceed customer expectations:

1. _____

2. _____

3. _____

Did you think of three things? If so, congratulations. If not, it's time to be proactive and think of ways your organization can delight customers. Share your ideas with upper management. They may or may not use your ideas, but at least you're doing your part to help your company succeed.

Next, write down three things you do to delight your employees:

1. _____

2. _____

3. _____

Did you think of three things? If so, congratulations. If not, it's time to start thinking of ways to delight your employees. Go out of your way to provide extra support. Think of ways to serve others. A manager who delights others within his or her organization will get a reputation as the "person to work for."

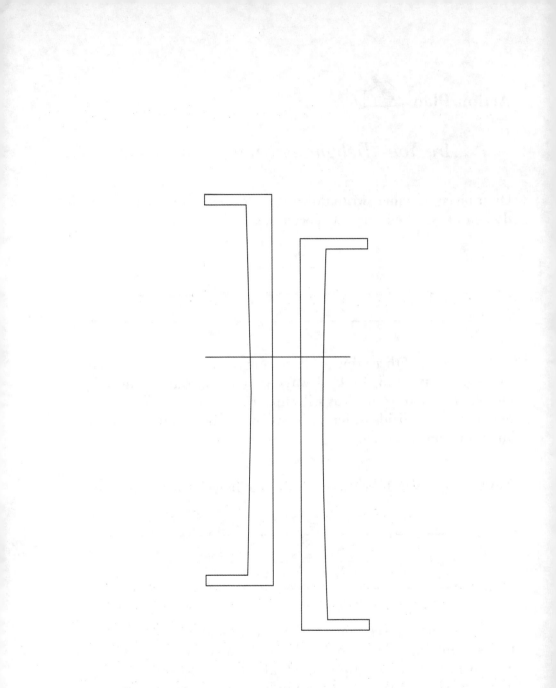

CHAPTER 3

The #1 Management Concept of All Time

In all my years as a manager and corporate trainer, I have yet to discover a more powerful management concept than the one I am about to share with you. During World War II General Patton was famous for employing this concept. Sam Walton, founder of Wal-Mart, built his reputation by doing this. Herb Kelleher, former CEO of Southwest Airlines and one of the most revered business leaders of our time, lived this concept every day. Hopefully your CEO and boss are both putting this concept into practice. I guarantee, if you start exercising this #1 concept every day in your department you will see an increase in performance, you will see better employee behavior, and you will begin to fulfill your #1 job as a manager.

What is the #1 Management Concept of All Time?

TURN THE PAGE TO FIND OUT! ☞

The Number One Secrets of Successful Managers

The #1 Management Concept of All Time Is...

MBWA

Management

by Wandering

Around

MBWA

You may have heard this acronym before. Executives at Hewlett-Packard developed this concept in the 1970s. In the 1980s, Tom Peters and Robert Waterman made the term even more popular. They discovered that managers who consistently interacted with employees and customers were more successful than managers who isolated themselves. Management by Wandering Around allows for informal communication and decreases the bureaucratic lines of communication. The best managers live this concept daily, reaping the rewards of time well spent.

So, what exactly is Management by Wandering Around? First, let us discover what MBWA is not.

What is NOT Management by Wandering Around

MBWA is NOT grabbing a cup of coffee in the morning and walking the halls for hours, chatting with everyone you see. That is a waste of corporate dollars.

MBWA is NOT micromanaging. Managers who constantly look over their employees' shoulders to check whether the work is being done will make them nervous. This results in decreased performance.

MBWA is NOT solving everyone's problems. Many managers spend too much time solving problems. Effective managers help employees find their own solutions.

What IS Management by Wandering Around

MBWA IS taking time out of your busy schedule to build relationships with employees.

MBWA IS giving employees consistent feedback on their performance.

MBWA IS soliciting feedback and listening to each employee's concerns and suggestions. MBWA affords managers the opportunity to build credibility and respect, and to take care of a potential problem early before it becomes a real problem.

Show your employees you are accessible to them. In his book, *The Heart of the Leader*, management expert Ken Blanchard says this: "True communication is making others feel safe." Your employees should feel safe around you and know that you have an ear bent in their direction. They should know you genuinely care about their welfare.

Get out and about. Ask your employees these questions now and then:

"What's on your mind?"

"What do you like about your department? What do you dislike?"

"If you could change something, what would you change?"

"Am I delivering the resources and training you need to do your job?"

As much as they are willing, talk to your employees about their personal lives. When appropriate, make notes to show the employee that you are not only listening, but also taking his or her job and personal development seriously.

Check In, Not Out

Managing by Wandering Around means checking IN with employees on a consistent basis, NOT checking them OUT constantly. You will drive your employees crazy if you constantly wander around getting feedback. Be consistent with your wandering around, not constant. Excellent managers occasionally get in the trenches with their employees, and sometimes do the dirty work.

Managers Who Did It Right

Because of this principle, General Patton's soldiers knew their leader cared. How did General Patton employ this concept during World War II? Many times General Patton could be found riding along with his soldiers as he led the advance through Germany. He didn't sit back in a safe place and let his troops do all the work. He put himself in harm's way many times to show his men that he was one of them.

Because of this principle, Sam Walton and Herb Kelleher's employees knew their leaders cared about them. Sam Walton and Herb

Kelleher were both known to fly around the country and meet their thousands of employees, reinforcing that they were important and part of a winning team.

MBWA Is Awareness

Be aware of what is going on with your employees. It's easy to get caught in the trap of work, work, work, and forget that it's the people, with their multitude of needs, that provide the quality products and services of your organization. You cannot afford to wear blinders and only see the task at hand.

Excellent managers are able to see what is going on in front of them and also see what's going on in the periphery. This means paying attention to subtle indicators, such as body language and nuances in the voice that can signal a potential problem. There should be few surprises in management.

Do you work in the kind of business where your employees do a lot of traveling? You can do your Management by Wandering Around by phone with employees who are out on the road. One-on-one is always best, but not always feasible. The sound of a caring voice at the other end of the phone can do wonders for an employee's morale.

Keep in Touch

It's easy to get caught up in your day-to-day duties and forget one of the primary rules in management: KEEP IN TOUCH WITH YOUR EMPLOYEES. It takes time, but it's the only way to build and maintain high morale and quality performance. Take to the halls and talk to people along the way. Visit people where they work. I can guarantee you'll reap great benefits by investing time now, instead of waiting to talk with your employees only when there are problems.

What is it like in the organization you work for? Does the head honcho show his or her face once in a while and ask you how you're doing? Does your boss manage by wandering around? Not only is it essential to the success and positive climate of any company, MBWA is the #1 management concept of all time.

The Number One Secrets of Successful Managers

Action Plan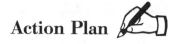

How Well Do You Know Your Employees?

On a piece of paper, write down the names of each employee you manage directly. Answer the following questions on each employee:

- *How does the employee feel about the job?*
- *What are the employee's strengths?*
- *What are the employee's weaknesses?*
- *What does the employee like about the job?*
- *What does the employee dislike about the job?*
- *When is the last time you asked the employee what he or she would like to see changed, and how did the employee respond?*
- *List at least three personal things you know about the employee, i.e. favorite sport, hobbies, marital status, etc.*

If you find you aren't writing much, then you must ask yourself how much you genuinely care about your employee's welfare and success. If you found you wrote a lot about a few employees and little on others, then ask yourself why. "Is there a personality conflict? Do I not like this person due to his or her beliefs, nationality, gender, habits, etc.?"

MBWA is a core management function. You must find the time to do it. The best managers do not do it because they have to, but because they want to. They know their employees are the foundation of both their personal success and the company's success.

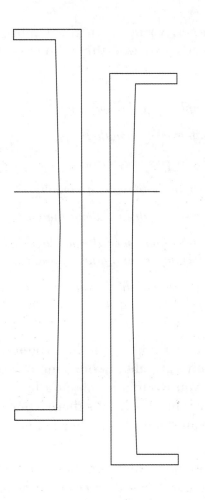

CHAPTER 4

The #1 Goal of Every Manager

Management is not easy. It is a place of privilege and a place of burden. A manager is like the lord of the manor who fulfills the wishes of the king or queen—I.e., the CEO. Managers do not have the luxury of sitting behind a desk all day giving orders for others to fulfill. Most managers today are working managers. Not only do they have mounds of work to do, they are also responsible for the mounds of work their employees must accomplish.

I am passing on to you the #1 goal of every manager as it was shared with me by a mentor I had while serving in the United States Air Force. The closer we each get to fulfilling this goal, the more our burden will be lightened. Not only is this a principle that will make your department more productive, this is a goal that can make your work more fulfilling.

If you think your job is to grind your hands to the bone every day to get high quality performance from your employees, you're wrong. That may be your reality when you first take over a new department, but it shouldn't last for months and months. In reality, the best way to fulfill your #1 job of making sure your employees are doing the jobs they were hired to do is to do everything within your power to reach this #1 goal.

What should be your #1 goal as a manager?

TURN THE PAGE TO FIND OUT! ☞

The Number One Secrets of Successful Managers

Your #1 Goal as a Manager Is to...

Work Yourself Out of a Job

Work Yourself Out of a Job

Wouldn't that be great? Wouldn't you love to get to the point where you are no longer needed? Is it possible? Yes! Is it probable? Not 100%, but you can get pretty close.

Managers are the glue; they keep things running smoothly. It is the employees who should be doing the bulk of the work.

The High Cost of Ignoring the #1 Goal of Every Manager

Managers who do not know how to get close to fulfilling this #1 goal are doomed to fatigue and possible burnout. They will find themselves living within a vicious cycle of constantly taking care of employee problems, all the while barely able to keep up with their own paperwork and other tasks. Sound familiar? Maybe you know a few managers who are living this vicious cycle. MAYBE YOU ARE EXPERIENCING THIS RIGHT NOW! If so, it's time to learn the lessons of this book.

Make Yourself Obsolete

"The best way to enjoy a management job is to be surrounded by people who don't need you anymore."

—HAL PITT

Managers must empower their employees and trust them to do the jobs they were hired to do. Managers need to retain the best employees—those who want to do a great job—weeding out those who do not want to accomplish the jobs they were hired to do.

In all my years of management, I have only met one person who believed he reached this goal 100 percent. After a management seminar in London, England, a man in his 60s told me he had reached the #1 goal of working himself out of a job. A top-level manager, he mentored his managers and employees to become leaders and take ownership for their performance and behavior. Those who did substandard work did not last long under his guidance. He demanded the best from each employee and would not tolerate poor performance. He said it took years, but he could honestly say he could go on a trip for a month and come back to a smooth running machine. The brightness in his eyes and the smile on his face persuaded me to believe him.

How can you make this happen in your department? What are the strategies you can use to ensure the majority of your employees are doing quality work and behaving professionally? How do you make yourself obsolete?

You already know one strategy: Management by Wandering Around. Giving and getting consistent feedback to and from employees. Meeting their training and resource needs. Doing everything within your power to help them succeed.

Creating Leaders Through the Theory of Critical Mass

A second powerful strategy to help work your way out of a job is the Theory of Critical Mass. This theory is used in thermodynamics to explain how explosion begets explosion. As applied to sociology, this theory explains how a few people who believe in a cause can influence a greater mass of people to believe in that same cause. The theory tells us:

*A minority of any society
can change that society.*

Famed anthropologist, Margaret Mead, said it like this:

> *"Never doubt that a small group of people can change the world."*

What does this theory mean to you as a manager? It means this: Once you develop strong leaders in your department or organization who are committed and have vision, those few will, in turn, develop other leaders. THAT means your job just got easier!

Are You Creating Leaders Through Your Leadership?

Be honest with the following questions to discover if you are employing the theory of critical mass in your organization:

> *"Do you have more leaders than followers in your department?"*

> *"Are you creating leaders who take up the mission and vision of the organization as their own?"*

> *"Do most of your employees continue to do an outstanding job when you are home sick or on vacation?"*

> *"Are you a dinosaur manager?"*

Dinosaur managers do not know how to create leaders. They want to hold onto the power and hoard the knowledge. They do not know how to delegate or how to empower employees. They are constantly checking OUT their employees instead of checking IN.

Critical mass leaders ultimately want to give away their power, allowing employees to take ownership of their own positions. Critical mass leaders get others excited about the mission and the vision of the organization by exuding passion and energy. Imagine the quality products and services an organization can provide if the people who staff it believe and act in accordance with the mission and vision of the organization. Imagine the quality products and services an organization can provide if the people who staff it take ownership of their own performance and behavior.

Putting the Theory of Critical Mass into Practice

It's one thing to see the importance of working yourself out of a job by creating leaders, quite another to know how to do it. Here's a practical way of putting the theory of critical mass to use.

Let's say you have ten employees. Set up a formal meeting with each employee individually to let them know you're willing to mentor them and help them become leaders in your department. Give your underachievers the benefit of the doubt. Let each employee know that by becoming a leader, they will not only help the department, but will also create a career path for themselves—promotion opportunities, raises, glowing performance evaluations.

Now it's time to set the example of excellence. Spend quality time with those employees who desire to become leaders. Mentor them by having occasional one-on-one training. Offer team training. Give them all some popular management resources to read. Have frequent meetings to coach and mentor. Praise them for their growth as leaders.

Yes, you will spend some of your personal time to accomplish this, but the payoff will make your efforts worthwhile. The best investments in life take time to build. You're on your way to working yourself out of a job.

As time progresses a few things will happen. First, the employees you are not giving as much quality time to will begin to complain. They may even say you're showing favoritism. Remind these employees that you are willing to mentor them and develop them into leaders. Remind them that your main goal as a manager is to build a strong organization grounded in excellence. Do not make these employees feel guilty. Treat all employees with respect and dignity. Continue to coach each employee fairly without any hint of favoritism.

The Evolution of Critical Mass Leaders

As time progresses, leaders will emerge in your department. They will serve as role models and their professional behavior will begin influencing other team members. In turn, they will take the time to mentor other employees to also become leaders.

Explosion will beget explosion and your small group of leaders will facilitate positive change in your department. Your team will become more synergistic and cohesive. Over time, you will have a department where 70 to 80 percent are self-directed leaders, empowered to take ownership of their own performance and hold other team members accountable for excellence. You will realistically reach your goal of being able to take a breath and relax. You will enjoy watching your team provide a consistent quality product and service to both internal and external customers without your even having to be there.

Does this sound too good to be true? I've talked with hundreds of managers who have facilitated this type of critical mass strategy to develop leaders in their departments and organizations.

One woman shared with me how her department experienced a dramatic shift from poor to good morale due to the persistent application of these principles by her new manager. She told me that her previous manager was ineffective and tyrannical, leaving morale in her department at an all-time low. The dinosaur manager was terminated for his ineffectiveness, and a new manager was hired to improve performance and "esprit de corps." The new boss took a month or so to get to know employees and the organizational environment, and then he began to mentor and coach. He managed by wandering around. He bought a well-known management book for each of his employees and set apart one hour a week to talk about it with his team. In six months the morale completely turned around and most of the employees were working harder than ever before. They actually had smiles on their faces, even though the job could be very stressful.

The High Payoff of Empowering Those You Manage

It is important to understand that each employee comes with a cost and a benefit. During initial employment, the cost of a new employee outweighs the benefit in terms of training, time, and other resources. As time progresses, each employee's benefit must begin to outweigh the initial and ongoing cost in terms of performance and behavior. If an employee's cost continues to outweigh the benefit to the team and the organization, that employee must be looked at closely.

If continued coaching and mentoring does not increase benefit over cost, it behooves the manager to decide whether that employee is a viable asset to the organization. It's a matter of investment. If money is the bottom-line – and time and effort equals money – it may not be in the best interests of the team and organization to continue investing in that employee. If coaching, mentoring, and discipline don't change the performance or behavior, it's time for that employee to find employment elsewhere. Your goal is to have leaders on your team.

Leadership Development Takes Time

Take leadership development slowly with each employee. Be discreet and do not hit your employees over the head with your enthusiasm. You will need to be aware of your employees' growth through Management by Wandering Around. Be willing to change your own behavior and grow through the process. Enjoy the long journey together. Changes in behavior do not happen overnight. Lasting behavioral changes only happen when someone sees the need to change. You must influence the employee to believe that personal change is good and necessary.

How far are you in reaching your #1 goal of working yourself out of a job? Are you creating leaders through effective coaching and mentoring? Try it. You will like it. And your persistence will pay off.

Action Plan

Create Leaders Through Critical Mass Thinking

On a piece of paper, write down the names of each employee you directly manage. Rate each employee on a scale of 1 to 5 (5 being the best) on how much of a leader he or she is within the department. For example, if you know 100% that the employee is doing quality work while you're on vacation, is acting as a team player, and is equipped to take care of problems that arise in your absence, that person is a 5.

Next to each employee's name, write down three ways you can begin developing that employee as a leader.

Next, set up a meeting with each employee and share your vision for your department. Tell them you would like to see them develop as leaders, both to enhance the department and to help their careers within the organization. Share the ideas you wrote down. Ask them three things they can do, either independently or with you, to develop their leadership skills.

Together, come up with a plan of action. Plan periodic meetings and follow-up.

Get ready for great things to happen. Be persistent, but don't be pushy, and give it time. Every person grows and changes differently. Some will develop into leaders easily and others will move more slowly. Reassess the action plan periodically.

Do not think you don't have time to do this. TAKE the time. Yes, you may put in long hours at first, but you will reap the benefits later and be proud of your accomplishments.

"Management isn't just a job. It's a lifetime commitment to other people's excellence."

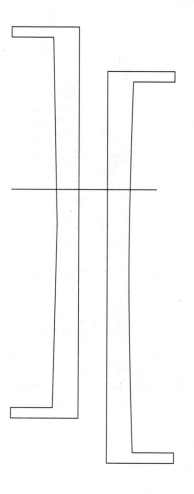

CHAPTER 5

The #1 Way to Reach Your #1 Goal

MBWA and the practical application of the theory of critical mass are two powerful strategies you can use to get maximum performance from your employees. They will aid you in working yourself out of a job. Using these strategies will put you ahead of the game, because many managers do not take the time to develop the leadership skills of others and do not take the time to get consistent feedback from employees.

There is another strategy you can use to reach your #1 goal of making your management job obsolete. I believe it is the #1 way of making your #1 goal a reality. It is a concept that's been around for a long time. In fact, it's one of the basic functions of management.

What is the #1 way to reach your #1 goal of working yourself out of a job?

TURN THE PAGE TO FIND OUT! ☞

The #1 Way to Reach Your Goal Is...

D.E.O.
Delegate, Empower, and Give Ownership

"A manager who does not delegate does not manage."

One of the primary functions of a manager is to delegate tasks, not do them. Even though managers are continually asked to do more with less, they must put teamwork and creativity to work, finding ways to hand off most of the tasks and projects to employees. Most employees want to do a good job and most desire responsibility.

What Delegation Is Not

Many managers use delegation inappropriately. Avoid the following abuses of delegation:

- Shirking responsibility that should be assumed by the manager
- Passing the buck to get out of doing a job
- Giving all the work to employees so the manager has more free time
- Giving employees tasks to accomplish without the authority to carry them out
- Constantly looking over an employee's shoulder to ensure he or she is doing the job correctly
- Holding on to most of the authority to avoid the risk of employee failure

What Delegation IS

Now that you know what ineffective delegation is, follow these steps to effective delegation:

- Transfer responsibility for a specific task or activity to the employee
- Give the employee clear direction on how to complete the task
- Give the employee the proper resources to complete the job

- Give the employee the power and authority to make the decisions necessary to complete the task
- Hold the employee accountable for completing the task
- Consistently check in with the employee to give and receive feedback concerning the task
- Take the consequences of employee failure so the employee does not become discouraged

The Benefits of Dynamic Delegation

To get our employees to buy into delegation, empowerment and ownership, we should have some good arguments as to why it is right for them and the department. Here are some benefits to delegation:

- Heightened productivity and quality
- Reduced costs
- More innovation and creativity from employees
- Improved customer service
- Greater commitment from the employees
- Increased employee decision-making skills
- Reduced stress for management

At Hewlett Packard, decision-making once took place only at the top levels of the organization. Being in a rapidly changing and highly competitive industry forced them to rethink the way they viewed management. Top management soon realized that the only way to survive was to delegate decision making to the lower ranks of the organization.

Hewlett Packard isn't the only company to rethink how it empowers its employees. Xerox, The American Society for Quality Control, and Federal Express are just a few examples of organizations that have found success through delegation and empowering employees.

What the Best Managers Know

*"If we don't delegate,
we fail our employees
and rob them of growth."*
—HAL PITT

There is more to management than putting out a quality product or service. The best managers are also involved in developing the skills and abilities of others. Delegation, empowerment, and ownership afford managers the opportunity of trusting their employees to do the jobs they were hired to do, by passing the authority and power to them. This is by far the best way for managers to work themselves out of a job. D.E.O. helps employees learn to make decisions on their own and to know the pains of failure and the joys of success.

*"It's a fine thing to have ability,
but the ability to discover
ability in others is the true test."*
—ELDER HUBBARD

The D.E.O. Process

1) Delegation

The D.E.O. process starts before you delegate a task or a project. There are Three Rights of Proper Delegation: Right Person, Right Resources, and Right Direction. The Right Person must be chosen before you begin.

• Right Person

Make sure the employee you choose has the experience and proper training to do the job. Some employees may never be right for a certain project. Know your employees' strengths and weaknesses. You may want to first obtain more training for the employee to ensure his or her success with the task or project. If at all possible, delegate tasks that challenge your employees. As the employee proves his ability to perform effectively in the job, he should be given tasks that are more complex and challenging.

• Right Resources

Get your employees the resources to do the job, or point them in the right direction as to where to get the resources. This means employees must have the supplies, equipment, budget, time and staffing to do the job. It is unfair to ask employees to do tasks or projects when they don't have the time or manning to do it right. It happens often in today's organizations and is a sign of inadequate functioning by top management. Do you remember the statistic? 80% of problems in organizations today are due to functional or structural inadequacies with management. Some organizations constantly run in crisis mode, dumping their crises in the laps of employees. Some of the "top brass" in organizations have not learned the art and science of time and project management, thus frustrating employees due to their own inadequacies.

A woman came up to me one day during a break in a seminar and said,

"Hal, I'm ready to quit, and so are my other ten employees."

"Why?" I asked.

"Well, our department is responsible for putting out lots of paper-work, and that means our employees need to be on computers constantly."

The woman sighed in frustration.

"Would you believe that our department has only ONE computer for the eleven of us? Management keeps telling us they don't have the budget for more computers and to just 'do our best.' Yet they badger us to produce more with less. I can't take it any more, and neither can my employees."

I wonder if that manager and the rest of the employees did quit. By not providing the proper resources, management was frustrating its employees and even keeping them from doing their jobs properly.

- **Right Direction**

Give your employees proper direction. Set a deadline, and mile-stones that must be met during the course of the project. Talk about standards, rules, policies, and guidelines that must be followed, and the result that the task or project must produce. Clearly communicate to the employee what is expected.

2) Empowerment

Once you've delegated (meaning you trust the employee to do the job because you've given him the right resources and direction to succeed), it's time to empower the employee. Empowerment means you give the employee the POWER and AUTHORITY to do the job however he wants! Empowerment means you relinquish control of the task or project and endow him with the authority to complete the task successfully.

When you empower employees, you usually empower them in the process, not the result. Each task or project has a certain objective that must be accomplished. But how the employee gets to that result is his business. Leave it in his capable hands. It can be hard to relinquish control and keep your hands off. But if you're going to get the best from your employees and not rob them of growth, it's time to keep your fingers out of the pie.

In their book, *Leadership: A Communication Perspective*, Hackman and Johnson give us four reasons why managers should give away power:

- **Increase task satisfaction and task performance.** People like their jobs more and work harder when they feel they have a significant voice in shaping decisions. By empowering employees, they will become more interested in their jobs and take even more pride in their work.

- **Greater cooperation among group members.** Sharing power fosters cooperation. Cooperation increases team accomplishment. Effective managers know how to combine individual efforts in order to achieve goals that would be beyond the capability of one person.

- **Group Survival.** Distributing power can save a company from failing in today's competitive environment. This gives employees the power to make quick decisions as market conditions change and also fosters creativity and innovation.

- **Personal growth and learning.** Effective managers help employees become more mature and productive. Empowerment is a key way to stimulate this growth. Through empowerment, employees learn new skills and find greater job satisfaction. This growth ultimately affects the whole department, as it has gained a more committed and skilled member.

With empowerment comes accountability. You must hold your employees accountable for completing the task. When there is accountability, employees understand that they must be able to explain their decisions and actions—and be willing to accept the consequences, whether favorable or unfavorable.

3) Ownership

The word "ownership" implies that one owns something. If you own a home, you are responsible for the upkeep. If you own a business, you are responsible for all aspects of running the business successfully.

When you empower your employees, you empower them in the PROCESS and hold them accountable for the results. When you give your employees ownership, you give them ownership of the PROGRAM. The more programs you can give to your employees, the closer you will be to working yourself out of a job.

When employees begin taking ownership of programs, the amount you have to delegate will be minimized. Employees will start managing various aspects of the department with very little supervision. Your role as a manager will become one of coach, mentor, and facilitator. Employees are held responsible for making decisions and solving problems.

A manager who worked in an education and training department learned the value of ownership. As a new manager, he found he always wanted to have his hands in everything and he delegated poorly. Since he rarely empowered his employees, he found himself working overtime and getting tired of the daily grind. At first, he blamed his employees for their lack of commitment. But by talking with other effective managers, he discovered he wasn't empowering his employees in the process or giving ownership over programs.

Soon he learned how to use the D.E.O. process effectively. He began delegating to his employees and empowering them. As time progressed and he learned the strengths of his employees, he began giving them ownership over programs. One employee was put in charge of scheduling. Another was given the responsibility of ordering supplies. Another was given ownership of the annual budget. And another was given the program of taking care of all the equipment. Within one year, his employees were running seventy percent of the department. He could go on vacation and have confidence that his department was running smoothly.

Check In Once in a While

Once you have delegated, empowered, and given your employees ownership over programs, don't turn your back and hope for the best. You must maintain some control. How much control depends upon a) the confidence you have in the employee's ability to complete the task, and b) the importance of the task. New employees in particular may need frequent feedback, while the more seasoned employee may need very little. No matter how much feedback you give the employee, make sure you make it clear that you aren't checking him out, but rather, checking in to see how things are going. You're asking for trouble when you never check in and fail to give timely feedback on progress, no matter how efficient the employee is at getting the job done. Everyone makes mistakes. It is your job as a manager to uncover those mistakes before they get out of control. This is where Management by Wandering Around comes in.

Powerful Story of Empowerment

A woman who worked for a major airline was sent to a company sponsored management course. The course emphasized the importance of empowerment and ownership. She was told that the airline wanted its employees to feel empowered to make good decisions that would affect the company in positive ways. Making customers happy was first priority. She was also taught that she didn't have to go hunt for a supervisor all the time to help the customer. She left the training believing she was empowered to make good decisions.

A few weeks later, a man stormed up and slammed his fist on the counter. He shouted, "Your airline just cancelled my flight to Italy and I have to be there in two days to speak to a large corporation. I don't know if you know who I am, but I'm the president of a billion-dollar company and I'm the keynote speaker. I must be in Italy in two days." He then pointed at the young woman and asked, "What are you going to do about it?"

The employee kept her cool and said, "Sir, no problem. I will get you to Italy on time."

She proceeded to book him flights on another airline and even had the resources to update his hotel accommodations. The man was impressed with her professionalism and outstanding customer service. He apologized for his behavior and left a happy man.

Unbeknownst to the employee, her supervisor was standing behind her and witnessed the whole event. He tapped her on the shoulder and asked her to step with him around the corner, where he gave her a verbal lashing.

"Who are you to make decisions like that? Don't you know you just cost this airline thousands of dollars by booking our customer with a competitor?"

The employee was confused by his harsh remarks. "But I just went to a training course a few weeks ago where I was taught that I'm empowered to make good decisions for the airline. That's what I did. He left very happy."

The supervisor stomped around for a few seconds and then put his face next to hers. "Well, don't ever let it happen again without asking me first."

The employee went back to work, feeling despondent and wary about the airline not practicing what it preached. She began making simple mistakes, uneasy that her supervisor might be looking over her shoulder.

A month later, her supervisor walked up with a letter that he asked her to read. The letter was from the CEO of the billion-dollar company to the CEO of the airline. It went something like this:

"Dear Sir, I'm writing this letter to thank you for the outstanding customer service I received from a Ms. Hudson one month ago. My flight to Italy was cancelled and I was very upset; I let the young lady know just how upset. She remained professional and polite and helped me rebook my flight with another airline. She even went out of her way to help change a few of my hotel arrangements. Because of the wonderful customer service I received from Ms. Hudson, I am giving your airline all of our company's business."

The young lady couldn't help but look up at her supervisor with a smile. She was not prepared for what the CEO wrote next.

"However, if I personally ever discover that Ms. Hudson has left your airline to work for another airline, we will take our business wherever she goes."

This is empowerment at its finest.

Empower Your Employees to Reach Your #1 Goal

A business is only as good as its empowered employees. The most successful businesses have learned that trusting and listening to employees and empowering them in the processes are some of the best ways to remain viable in today's competitive economy.

Start delegating and empowering your employees. Give them ownership over programs. They will be happier and more productive at work. Most employees want to be delegated to and then left alone. Employees hate to be micromanaged. They want to be trusted to do the jobs they were hired to do. I guarantee that if you delegate, empower, and give ownership for tasks and projects to your employees, you'll soon find that you are relaxing more at work, enjoying management, and moving toward your #1 goal of working yourself out of a job.

Action Plan – Take Time to Reflect

Do You Delegate To and Empower Your Employees?

The following questions will help you reflect on your ability as a manager.

- Do you take responsibility for your own work and not pass the buck to get out of doing your job? .... ❏ Yes ❏ No

- Do you freely give your employees the power and authority to carry out tasks? .... ❏ Yes ❏ No

- Do you refrain from constantly looking over an employee's shoulder to ensure he or she is doing the job correctly? .... ❏ Yes ❏ No

- Do you delegate, even though you think you can do the job better? .... ❏ Yes ❏ No

- Are you unafraid of losing your power and authority by giving it to others? .... ❏ Yes ❏ No

- Do you hold your employees accountable for the completion of tasks? .... ❏ Yes ❏ No

- Are you willing to take the extra time to train an employee on a task instead of doing it yourself to save time? .... ❏ Yes ❏ No

- If a task is completed correctly and on time, are you happy, even though it may not have been the way YOU would have completed it? ❏ Yes ❏ No

- Do you do everything within your power to obtain for your employees the resources they need to do the task? . . . . ❏ Yes ❏ No

- Do you give clear direction as to what standards and guidelines must be met during any given task or project? . . . . ❏ Yes ❏ No

- Do you give clear direction as to the specific results you want to achieve with the task or project? . . . . ❏ Yes ❏ No

Every employee is different (some may not be ready for empowerment with a specific task or project) but each "yes" will bring you closer to your #1 goal—to work yourself out of a job by creating leaders in your department.

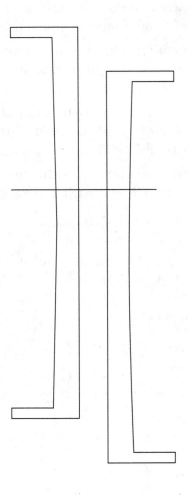

CHAPTER 6

The #1 Attitude
Every Manager Must Have

Our attitudes govern the way we behave toward certain situations and people. We may not be able to control the events around us, but we can control the way we think about and respond to those events.

In a business environment, we cannot control someone's inward attitude. We cannot demand that employees come to work with positive, enthusiastic attitudes. It's up to the individual how he or she chooses to view the world. Yet managers must strive to exude a certain attitude at work. This #1 attitude is the cornerstone of building effective relationships and high credibility within an organization. Without this attitude, managers will find it hard to motivate, inspire, and gain commitment from their employees. The right attitude helps us set a standard of excellence for others to follow.

What is the #1 attitude that managers must have to succeed in their organizations?

TURN THE PAGE TO FIND OUT! ☞

The Number One Secrets of Successful Managers

The #1 Attitude Every Manager Must Have Is...

A

Professional

Attitude

Effective Managers Command Respect

A manager who exudes a professional attitude at work is sure to command respect from most employees and the top brass. Having this attitude is one of the best ways to build a career and get promoted. In fact, those responsible for promoting employees should seriously consider NOT promoting an individual to a management or supervisory position who does not possess the following asset: a strong reputation amongst subordinates and peers for having a professional attitude. Organizations need managers who can be the glue to hold departments together.

An organization MUST require that all its members exhibit professional behavior toward external and internal customers. There are no excuses for the kind of poor behavior that can have a detrimental effect on creating and retaining customers.

Key Characteristics of a Professional Attitude

Let's take a look at some of the key characteristics of managers who exude a professional attitude:

- Professional managers treat everyone with dignity and respect. They believe that employees are the most important resource in the organization and accordingly treat them like gold. Screaming and abusive language should not be tolerated.

- Professional managers are predictable. There's nothing worse than having a boss who comes to work in a good mood one day and ready to cut everyone's head off the next. This Jekyll and Hyde behavior confuses and alienates employees and can ruin a manager's credibility. A professional manager learns to control his emotions and knows where to go to vent when he needs to.

- Professional managers are proactive. They take the bull by the horns and make things happen. They are consistently part of the solution, not the problem.

- Professional managers exude a positive attitude. They don't tolerate whiners and negativity. They don't spend time standing around the water cooler speaking poorly about the organization, upper management, or fellow employees.

- Professional managers invest in their employees. In his book, *The Seven Habits of Highly Effective People*, Stephen Covey gives a wonderful analogy of how managers can get maximum performance from employees. He says we should view our employees as if they were piggy banks. Every day we invest certain currencies in them. These currencies are: the penny of understanding, the nickel of compassion, the dime of clear direction, the quarter of sincerity, and the dollar of professionalism. When we invest these currencies in our employees, we build trust and respect. When we invest these currencies, most employees will want to do an outstanding job for both the manager and the team. However, if we invest in our employees the penny of disrespect, the nickel of overreacting, the dime of betraying their trust, the quarter of insincerity, and the dollar of behaving unprofessionally, we will go BANKRUPT as managers.

Take time to invest in your employees. You reap what you sow. Great managers know that before they can ask for the hand, they must win the heart. When you build a bank account of trust and respect with your employees, you have something to draw upon when it comes time to delegate, deal with conflict, or confront a performance issue.

> "*Winning the confidence of your people now may well be invaluable in a yet-unforeseen time when you face your ultimate test. No one can know when that day will come or even if it will. But if it does, early investment in winning support among even your most stalwart opponents may make the difference between success and defeat when it counts most.*"
>
> —MICHAEL USEEM

- Professional managers are enthusiastic about being managers. They realize that organizations run on energy and they supply that energy to reach the mission and vision of the organization. Their passion for excellence is contagious.

It's important to note that being enthusiastic doesn't mean you have to jump around and do cartwheels. Some people show their enthusiasm more overtly than others. Mother Teresa was considered to be one of the most enthusiastic individuals one could ever meet. Even though she was quiet and soft-spoken, she exuded an energy that let those around her know she was on a crusade and that she strongly believed in the good cause of helping the poor and homeless. Let others catch the enthusiasm of your belief in your employees, your department, and the organization.

- Professional managers know the importance of forming interpersonal linkages with others. Because it is so powerful in its impact on us as managers, I have devoted Chapter 18 to this concept. Suffice it to say for now that it is vitally important to get to know other people in your organization.

- Professional managers don't procrastinate over unpleasant duties.

"Successful people form the habit of doing what failures don't like to do. They like the results they get by doing what they don't necessarily enjoy."

—EARL NIGHTENGALE

Some jobs are tedious, monotonous, and boring. Be the person who stands up to bat and says "I can do this" or "I'm willing to take a shot at that." Gain a reputation as a "can-do" person who doesn't shirk the unpleasantness of life.

- Professional managers are fair and consistent in their dealings with employees. No favoritism allowed.

There is nothing more unfair than the equal treatment of unequal employees.

Give employees what they deserve. Hold all to the same high standards of quality work, and be fair across the board. Your good, hard working employees deserve positive reinforcement for their work. The ones who let other employees down or who don't do what is required of them do not deserve the rewards given to employees with higher standards. We must hold each accountable for doing the jobs they were hired to do.

- Professional managers are not overly concerned if some employees don't like them. They desire to be surrounded by people who want to do quality work.

"I'd much rather deal with someone who's good at their job but malevolent toward me, than someone who likes me but is a ninny."

–SAM DONALDSON

Set the Example of Excellence

Attitudes are contagious. Set the example of excellence and watch your employees catch your good attitudes.

Action Plan—Take the Professionalism Test

Are You Behaving Like a Professional at Work?

Below are 10 questions. Each is worth a maximum of 10 points. Take the test and discover the areas of professionalism you are living right now, as well as those areas where you can do better.

	Not Very Often	*Some of the Time*	*Most of the Time*
	1	5	10

1. I treat all people with dignity and respect	1	5	10
2. I am predictable in my behavior	1	5	10
3. I am a proactive, solution-oriented person	1	5	10
4. I have a positive mental attitude	1	5	10
5. I invest positively in my employees' bank accounts	1	5	10

6. I exude a passionate, enthusiastic attitude	1	5	10
7. I take time to develop interpersonal linkages	1	5	10
8. I am willing to take on unpleasant duties	1	5	10
9. I am fair and consistent in my treatment of employees	1	5	10
10. I am not in management for a popularity contest	1	5	10

Total up the numbers. How did you do?

90–100 = A   80–89 = B   70–79 = C   60–69 = D

Under 60 = lots of work to do

Total _____

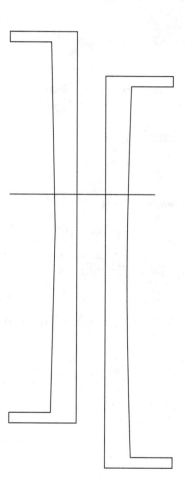

CHAPTER 7

The #1 Way to Motivate and Retain Most Employees

Across the U.S.A., managers in my seminars ask me these questions: "How do I motivate my employees?" and "How do I retain my best employees?"

If you've been asking yourself these questions about your own employees, you're not alone. In 2000, Coca-Cola, Strouds, Macy's, and Nordstrom were asking the same questions about their own employees. These large companies wanted to know how to retain their best employees and how to motivate them to do the jobs they were hired to do. Through employee polls and surveys, and by consulting with outside agencies, they attempted to find answers to employee retention and motivation.

Once the results were tallied, something remarkable happened. Independent of one other, these companies uncovered the same truth. Of the thousands surveyed, most employees said there was ONE THING more than any other that would motivate them to do a good job and stay with their companies.

Are you ready for their answer? Do you want to find out what you can do to motivate and retain most of your employees? Get ready! What you're about to learn is earth shattering! Before you turn the page, ask yourself

What do you think is the #1 way to retain and motivate most employees?

TURN THE PAGE TO FIND OUT! ☞

The Number One Secrets of Successful Managers

The #1 Way to Motivate and Retain Most Employees Is to...

Show Appreciation for a Job Well Done

Show Appreciation for a Job Well Done

Simply by praising your employees, you can motivate and retain most of them. What those billion dollar companies discovered was that employees want to feel valued. They want to know that their efforts are making a difference.

Polls and Surveys Reveal the Truth About Appreciation

Through the years, there have been hundreds of studies conducted on employee motivation and retention. When it comes to what employees desire more than anything else, praise and appreciation for a job well done almost always rate the highest. Not money. Not promotions. PRAISE!

In a nationwide survey of 2,000 workers conducted by the Gallup Organization and Carlson Marketing Group, 69 percent of employees said they find praise and recognition from their bosses more motivating than money. Four out of five said recognition and praise motivates them to do a better job.

Now, I'm a believer in polls and surveys, but what convinces me is my own experience. In many of my seminars, I ask those in attendance to write down the #1 thing their organizations can do to motivate them and keep them with the company. Of the thousands who have attended my seminars through the years, most of them—regardless of gender, age, or nationality—give me similar answers, such as:

> *"Just recognize my efforts. Tell me I'm doing a good job once in a while."*

> *"Make me feel valued and let me know that I am doing things right."*

> *"Show me you appreciate me."*

> *"I work hard every day and it feels good when my boss lets me know once in a while that my work is appreciated."*

If millions and millions of employees want to hear praise and to feel appreciated where they work, then know that the same is true of YOUR EMPLOYEES. They want to feel appreciated for the hard work they do for YOU.

Do you praise your employees? Are you SHOWING THEM how much they're appreciated? Do you recognize their hard work? I sometimes hear this in my seminars: "I have low morale among my employees. What can I do?" I always ask that person, "Do you have a corporate culture of praise and recognition in your company? Do your employees feel valued and appreciated?" Many companies suffer from low morale because the top brass and middle management forget that it's their employees who get the work done. They take their employees hard efforts for granted.

Practical Ways to Show Appreciation

Showing appreciation for a job well done is the #1 way to motivate and retain most employees. Below is a list of some practical things you can start doing now to SHOW your employees you appreciate them.

- Catch your Employees Doing Something Right. It is so easy to focus on the problem areas and forget all the great work employees are doing. Get in the habit of looking for the positives. The more good you look for, the more good you will find.

- Birthday Cards. Send birthday cards to those employees you directly manage. They will appreciate it.

- Thank You Cards. Send a thank you card to your employees once in a while. A&G Merchandising Company in Delaware reduced turnover by giving team leaders specially printed packets of thank you cards to help recognize those employees who do exceptional work.

- Specific Verbal Praise. Telling employees "You're doing a good job" isn't enough. Praise should be detailed and relevant. Use phrases such as:

"You did a great job on..."

"You've really made a difference by..."

"I'm impressed with..."

When you praise, make sure you don't sandwich it between slices of criticism. The employee is more likely remember the criticism.

- Public Recognition. There is an old adage, "Praise in public, criticize in private." Recognize your hard workers in front of others.

- Third Party Praise. Tell your employees how much you appreciate your other employees. In his book, *Make Peace With Anyone*, David Lieberman gives us this great advice:

"To adjust anyone's thinking about you, tell a third party—maybe a mutual friend—what it is that you honestly like and respect about this person, or tell them how you admire her for something she's done or even stands for. Whether it's a coworker, boss, assistant, neighbor, sibling, child, mechanic—everyone needs to feel appreciated. Let this third party know your genuine warm feelings toward her and watch the magic happen. When we hear something from a third party, we rarely question the veracity of what we're told."

Everyone Wants to Feel Appreciated

Sometimes in my seminars I hear this: "Come on, birthday cards? Thank you cards? Isn't that a little much? I work in construction with a bunch of men who could care less about this praise stuff."

Before you dismiss these simple ways of showing appreciation, let me tell you of an encounter I had a few years ago.

I was in Massachusetts one Saturday getting ready to give a workshop on management to a group of union machinists. Around twenty men walked in and sat down. I looked around the room and gulped. Most of these men didn't seem too happy to be there. Many of them looked like Grizzly Adams with long beards and tough exteriors. Most were big enough to squash me with one bicep.

About an hour into the workshop, with very little feedback from the group, I started talking about the importance of praise and recognition. I decided not to spend too much time on birthday and thank you cards, thinking that these were tough union machinists who probably could care less about such things. They might view cards as too touchy-feely. So I mentioned birthday cards and the importance of praise, intending to move quickly onto another subject.

Then something happened that I didn't see coming. A man with a long gray beard raised his hand and said, "Hal, I just want to tell you that my boss sent me a birthday card a couple of weeks ago. I sure did appreciate it."

Another man raised his hand, stating that he had received a thank you card from his boss, which he also appreciated. Yet another man raised his hand to share how his boss praised him all the time. Then another man, and another, and another—each affirming how he had received some form of praise or appreciation for a job well done.

Here were men I thought of as macho, laughing together about how their company makes them feel special. I was given a reality check that day. If a two hundred pound union worker who looks like Grizzly Adams cares about getting a birthday or thank you card, then I guarantee your employees will appreciate the same.

Praise Does Not Cost Much

Praise is an inexpensive but powerful way to keep morale high and production going strong. One moment spent sharing a good word can translate into hours of high productivity.

Action Plan

Rate How Praise Is Used in Your Company

Praise and appreciation are too important to overlook or neglect.

Assess your organization in terms of a culture of praise and recognition.

Does top management let employees know how valued they are? Below, rate your organization on a scale of 1 to 5 (5 being the best).

Top management praises employees regularly: 1 2 3 4 5

Top management has recognition programs: 1 2 3 4 5

Top management exhibits behaviors that
    show employees they are valued: 1 2 3 4 5

If top management rated high, you probably work in a great environment. If not, your organization may be experiencing low morale and substandard performance from some employees.

Now it's time to assess yourself as a manager. Rate yourself using the method given above:

You praise your employees regularly: 1 2 3 4 5

You recognize your hard workers: 1 2 3 4 5

You exhibit behaviors that show your
    employees how valued they are: 1 2 3 4 5

How did you rate as a manager? If you find you aren't praising and recognizing your employees' hard work, it's time to start. Take responsibility for your own leadership and find ways to build a culture of praise and recognition in your department. As you develop a great department, the word on the grapevine will say that you are the person to work for.

CHAPTER 8

The #1 Way to Motivate
EVERY Employee

In the last chapter, we learned that appreciation for a job well done is the #1 way to motivate and retain MOST employees. Yet some employees aren't all that interested in receiving praise. They don't mind being recognized, but it's really not that big of a deal.

A young man who worked in a high tech company once told me, "Hal, I don't care much about being praised for doing a good job. As long as I know within myself that I'm doing a good job, that's all that matters. But get me a bigger computer monitor and a faster hard drive with lots of memory—that's what will motivate me to stay in my company."

If praise and appreciation won't motivate every employee, then how can we know what will? If you're like me, you spent years busting your head against the wall attempting to motivate your employees using all kinds of strategies. Some worked on some employees and some not at all.

Is there a way to inspire all of our employees? Is there some magic we can use to motivate all of our employees toward peak performance? Yes, there is! I wish I'd learned this strategy early in my management career; it would have saved me from years of frustration.

This strategy is so simple, so elementary, yet it has eluded even the most seasoned managers. Sometimes the best strategies are right under our noses, but we don't see them until someone points them out. Let me save you some considerable frustration by revealing

What is the #1 way to motivate
every one of your employees?

TURN THE PAGE TO FIND OUT! ☞

The Number One Secrets of Successful Managers

The #1 Way to Motivate Every Employee Is to...

Ask Them

Ask, and You Shall Be Told

Yes, it's that simple. ASK THEM! Why spend years trying to learn what motivates your employees when THEY WILL TELL YOU! As you'll learn in another chapter, asking questions is the most powerful communication strategy we have at our disposal. Unless you're a mind reader, there is only one way to find out what motivates your employees: sit down with each one and ask what motivates them.

The Motivation Sheet

This brings us to the practical strategy we can employ to get this done. It's called the motivation sheet. Let me explain what it is by way of example.

A manager who works in an organization of over 500 employees shared with me the story of how the motivation sheet impacted her department.

Morale was poor and the organization had not been getting the results it needed to stay competitive. The CEO happened to learn about the importance of asking employees what motivates them, and he decided to introduce the motivation sheet to his management team.

The organization generated its own sheet on a computer. The layout was simple: a line for the employee's name, another for the date, and a column for employees to list the top ten things their company could do to motivate and retain them. The manager who related the tale to me received twelve copies of the motivation sheet for the twelve employees in her department. Now it was time to act.

She met with each of her employees and asked them to list on the sheet the top ten things the company could do to motivate and retain them. Some employees could think of ten, some four or five. One older woman could think of only two things: appreciation for a job well done and Kit Kat candy bars.

The manager collected the motivation sheets, studied them, and put them in a file labeled The Motivation Sheet File. She then did everything she could to fulfill what each employee had listed. For the Kit Kat woman, now and then she bought a small package of Kit

Kats to leave on her desk while the employee was away. She also placed a sticky note on the candy bar package, letting the employee know how much she was appreciated. The manager began to see small changes in the elderly employee's behavior and performance. She seemed happier in her job.

When it came time for the Kit Kat woman's performance review, the manager asked her if there was anything on the motivation sheet she would like to change. This is important—people's needs change, as do their motivators. The employee smiled and said, "Honey, as long as you keep giving me those Kit Kats, I'll never quit."

Kit Kats. Can you believe it? That's what motivated one employee. The manager discovered that different things motivated each employee. She discovered that 70 percent of the employees listed praise and recognition as their main motivator. One employee listed more challenging work as her #1 motivator and feeling empowered as #2 on the list. Another employee said being given clear direction was his #1 motivator. Another said getting the resources to do the job was #1.

The manager said that the motivation sheet brought about remarkable changes in the performance and behavior of her employees, and within six months the entire organization seemed like a different place. Employees were happier and results in many areas were exceeding expectations. This all came about because the CEO discovered the importance of asking employees what can be done to retain and motivate them.

I challenge you to try the motivation sheet in your organization. It works. Why? Because employees feel more loyalty to an organization that makes it a point to meet their needs.

What if an employee lists a raise as his or her #1 motivator, but a raise is out of the question because your organization only considers raises on an annual basis? Or what if an employee lists a desire so far-fetched it can't possibly be met? Then be honest. Remind the employee how raises are awarded in your organization. Let the employee know that if he or she continues performing well, you'll go to bat for them at the annual review.

As manager, you must decide what is feasible. That's why you want the employee to list more than one desire on the motivation sheet. If you can't meet the #1 need, then go to #2 or #3 and do everything you can to meet a need that will motivate your employee.

Negotiate to Meet Employee Needs

Here's another example of how simply asking your employees can make a difference. A manager asked a new employee in an emergency room what would motivate her. Janice said she wanted to go to college more than anything in the world. After some negotiating, the manager told Janice she could sign up for the classes she wanted to take, but she would have to make a concession. She would have to work almost every weekend. Janice was ecstatic to be college-bound and said that working weekends was fine.

The manager needed to negotiate the employee's #1 motivator. If he allowed the employee to go to college AND get the same time off as the other employees, some of her peers might have screamed favoritism. By negotiating with Janice on her #1 motivator, the manager killed two birds with one stone. He now had a motivated employee who was living her dream, as well as other happy employees getting more weekends off.

You Won't Make Everyone Happy

One important note about asking employees what motivates them: YOU WON'T MAKE EVERYONE HAPPY. There are always going to be those few employees who, no matter what you do, will never be happy. And that's fine. Let them be unhappy. They are still required to behave professionally, delight customers, and do the job they were hired to do. If they don't like it, they can go get a job somewhere else.

Ask your employees what motivates them. Do everything within your power to meet their needs. You will benefit greatly by having motivated employees who will perform well and want to stick around during hard times.

Action Plan — Try This for Fun

Before you employ the motivation sheet in your department, talk with your boss or upper management about the benefits of the motivation sheet. If management balks at the idea, ask if you can use it in your department on a trial basis. At least you can find out what motivates your employees and try to meet those needs.

Meanwhile, try this for fun. Start asking people in your organization what their #1 motivator is.

> ### *"If I was your boss,*
> ### *what is the #1 thing I could do to motivate you*
> ### *and retain you in our organization?"*

Ask as many people as you can, and write down what they say. What you discover may amaze you. You'll find that there are more people than you realized who simply want to be appreciated, empowered, challenged, and given clear direction on what's expected of them. You'll discover that money is not what motivates most employees.

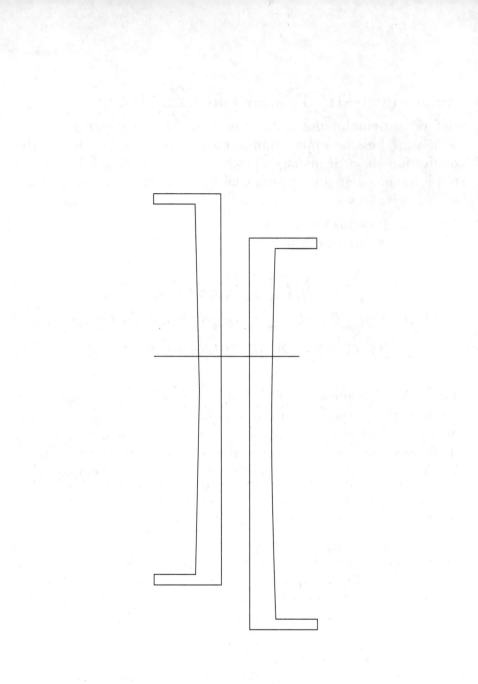

CHAPTER 9

The #1 Way to Gain Employee Commitment

Are most of your employees committed to you and the department you run? Are they committed to the vision and mission of the organization? Or do many of them do the bare minimum required to earn their paychecks?

One of the greatest challenges for any manager is gaining employee commitment. We all want employees who are enthusiastic about delighting customers, employees who believe in the products and services our organizations provide. We learned in the last few chapters how praise and showing appreciation can motivate and retain employees. But praise and recognition aren't enough. I can praise employees all day and still not gain their commitment.

Most employees desire a certain ingredient as part of the management stew. This is the #1 ingredient for gaining employee commitment. If you find that you're having a hard time in this area, help is just the flip of a page away.

What is the #1 way to gain employee commitment?

TURN THE PAGE TO FIND OUT! ☞

The #1 Way to Gain Employee Commitment Is...

Involvement

Ask, Don't Tell

If you want to get employees committed to your department, it's time to get them involved in the decision-making processes. Empower them to start making smart decisions, and hold them accountable for the results.

A sure-fire way to breed an under-performing department is for the manager to make all of the decisions, and to consistently TELL employees what to do and how to do it. I don't know about you, but I dislike being TOLD what to do by my boss. I can't stand a boss who circles like a hawk, watching my every move. I want to be given clear direction, the resources to do the job, and then be set free to fly on my own.

Like you, I want to have a say in my destiny. A recent study revealed that 77 percent of employees desire freedom at work – freedom to make smart choices that will have a positive impact on the bottom line.

Are you a dictatorial manager who likes to hold the reins and tell people what to do? If so, good luck gaining the respect and commitment of your employees. Employees don't generally like to be told what to do. Employees in today's society like to be ASKED what to do. It's called democracy.

Attract the Best Employees Through Empowerment and Involvement

The smartest managers today have realized that to attract the best employees, empowerment and involvement in decision-making must be a value of the organization. Here's what Colin Powell had to say on this subject in 1999 when he spoke to Sears employees in New York:

"Organization doesn't really accomplish anything. Plans don't accomplish anything either. Theories of management don't much matter. Endeavors succeed or fail because of the people involved. Only by attracting the best people will you accomplish great deeds. In a brain-based economy, your best assets are people. We've heard this expression so often that it's become trite. But how many leaders really 'walk the talk' with this stuff? Too often, people are assumed to be empty chess pieces to be moved around by grand viziers, which may explain why so many top managers immerse themselves in the goal of creating an environment where the best, the brightest, the most creative are attracted, retained, and, most importantly, unleashed."

Unleash the potential of your employees as Colin Powell challenges us to. Give them the chance to be creative and innovative. Let them revel in an environment where they are ASKED about better ways to delight customers, or ASKED how to make a product or service better. When management really listens, it may well discover that employees can help management see things it may have missed.

Develop Leaders Through Involvement and Accountability

Involve your employees in the day-to-day operations of the department. Get them involved in the empowerment process of delegation. Allow them the flexibility to try new things. Allow them the opportunity to fail. Shape them into leaders who will take ownership of their own performance and behavior.

Employees will automatically become more committed when they feel they have a stake in the outcome.

A mission imposed is a mission opposed.

Don't impose your will on your employees or they'll distrust you. Again, we live in a democratic society where the people have a voice. The same is true in our organizations. Employees want to feel free to voice their suggestions and concerns without threat of retaliation. They want to be heard.

People rise to the challenge when
it's their challenge.

I'm no exception. I have a hard time getting excited when my boss hands me some work and says, "Do it this way." I do, however, get excited when my boss challenges me with a task or project and then asks, "Do you see a better way of doing this?" My boss's challenge has now become my challenge. Whenever I've been empowered in the process, I will be more apt to take pride in reaching the desired result.

Practical Ways to Gain Employee Commitment

Here are a few practical ways we can get our employees more involved and gain their commitment:

- Monthly team meetings. Instead of holding meetings strictly for the dissemination of information, set aside a portion of the meeting so that team members can voice their opinions and concerns. Ask questions such as: "What can we do next month to get even greater results?" or "What can we do next month to make morale even better than last month?" Make sure you follow up on their feedback.

- The Suggestion Box. Dedicate a company e-mail address or suggestion box to solicit employee feedback. Let employees know you're looking for policies, procedures, or problems that could be causing people to leave the company.

- Have one-on-one sessions with your employees. Get together with each individual once in a while and ask how he or she feels about the department and what could be done better. Ask questions, listen to what the employee has to say, and then follow through the best that you can. This is Management by Walking Around in action.

- Get employees involved in solutions. When an employee has a good idea, give him the responsibility to follow through. Create a proactive, solution-oriented spirit. You'll be surprised at the amount of employees who are willing to take the initiative just because they were asked and then finally listened to. This is also a great way to keep the whiners quiet. They know that if they come to you with a gripe you'll put some, if not all, of the responsibility back on them to devise a solution.

- Answer the question "WHY?" Many employees need to know the significance behind tasks and procedures. They want to know their actions will have an impact. Employees have every right to ask managers why certain things are done. Of course, a few employees can drive us crazy asking millions of questions. It is still important to answer their questions to the best of our ability. Never say this: "Because I said so!" Such statements stifle commitment and can ruin our credibility. There may be times you do not know the answer to the question. You may need to say something like this: "Bill, at this time the CEO hasn't explained to me why we're engaged in this project, but it is something she wants done by Friday. Let's put our heads together and find the best way to get this done."

- Get your employees involved in your management. This is a great way to gain employee commitment. I know of hundreds of managers who have tried this strategy, and it works.

In the last chapter we talked about the motivation sheet. There is another sheet you'll want to have on each of your employees. It's called The Management Sheet. Meet with each of your employees and ask them these questions: "What can I do for you as a manager in this department?" and "What type of management style do you find helps you accomplish your job?"

You'll be amazed at what you discover. You will find that each employee perceives management differently and desires certain things from a manager. I do this exercise in all my management workshops. I have each attendee ask five other attendees what they look for from their bosses. The answers are as varied as the stars in the sky.

> *"Give me space. Don't look over my shoulder and I'll do a great job."*
>
> *"Just show me you appreciate me once in a while."*
>
> *"Empower me and get me involved in the department."*
>
> *"Get me the resources I need to do my job."*
>
> *"Give me clear direction on tasks and projects."*
>
> *"Let me know where I stand in the department. Don't surprise me one day by telling me I'm not doing my job."*
>
> *"Help me build a career in the department so I can get promoted."*
>
> *"Let me talk with you once a week about how I think things are going in the department."*

Involvement is the Key to Commitment

Involvement. It's the #1 way to gain employee commitment. Create a sense of loyalty in your employees by showing them that their actions will benefit themselves and the company. Show them their suggestions and questions are valued. Set the example of excellence by being committed to helping your company fulfill its #1 purpose – that is, to create and retain customers.

Action Plan—Time for Reflection

Do You Get Your Employees Involved?

Think about yourself as a manager right now. Think about how you behave toward your employees at work.

Are you the type of person who asks questions and gets others involved in decision-making?

Or do you make most of the decisions yourself and expect compliance?

Remember that you won't always have the answers. That's why you need others to help you see what you might be missing. Don't be too proud to ask employees if they see a better ways of doing things. It's the smart thing to do. In fact, in today's competitive economy, it's the only way to truly grow a business.

I challenge you to ask each of your employees what they're looking for from you as a manager. Do this within a few weeks. It's a great strategy to meet the management needs of your employees.

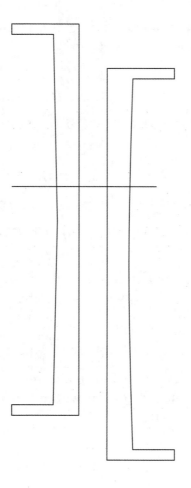

CHAPTER 10

The #1 Reason Most Employees Quit

Ever wonder why people quit their jobs? Have you ever quit a job before? There are dozens of reasons people quit organizations, but recent studies have revealed one main factor that contributes to most employees leaving their companies.

When I ask this question in my workshops, more than half the participants get the answer right away.

What do you think the #1 reason most employees quit their jobs is?

TURN THE PAGE TO FIND OUT! ☞

The Number One Secrets of Successful Managers

The #1 Reason
Most Employees Quit Is...

They Quit
Lousy Bosses

The Statistics and Professionals Speak

Ouch! The main reason employees quit is because of us—the managers, the bosses—the glue that is supposed to hold the organization together. Below are some statistics and quotes about employees quitting ineffective bosses:

A recent management study of 500 professional employees by Mastery Works in Annandale, Virginia, revealed that the primary factor affecting a respondent's decision to leave an organization was whether or not the manager developed a trusting relationship with him.

> *"One of the main reasons people quit their jobs is because they dislike the manager."*
>
> —KELLY GILMORE

Tom Davenport of Towers Perrin, an international management consulting firm, tells us this:

> *"There is an enormous correlation between an employee's job performance and the effectiveness of his or her manager. If HR can build the capability of line managers, they will build performance and satisfaction levels."*

When people quit, it's important for the top brass to discover why. What they'll discover is that management may not be doing it right, all the way from the CEO to midline supervisors. Just because a person has built a multi-million dollar company does not mean that person knows how to manage and lead people. It may be that person merely has an uncanny business sense. Just look at the business news in your paper or on television. Story after story tells us of CEOs and managers who were unethical or unprofessional.

What do all of these statistics and quotes from the professionals in management have to do with us? Simply this: we need to be doing it right! We want to build ourselves into EXCEPTIONAL MANAGERS, so our employees will think twice before quitting us.

Learn From the Best How to Do It Right

Fortunately for us, we have shining examples of managers and CEOs who are doing things right. We have people we can model ourselves after so we can be exceptional bosses. Let's take a look at just a few exceptional men and women who do it right:

Fred Manske, Jr. is CEO of Purolator Courier, Canada's largest distribution company. He tells us why he believes he has been so successful:

> *"The No. 1 reason I got to where I am today is my desire to help my colleagues and employees. I've always had peers who supported me, because I was unselfish with them. The best way to be successful is to serve others by observing and emulating acts you admire in leaders. Look for examples both inside and outside your organization. Then make a sincere effort to show that you're unselfish."*

Harvey MacKay, author of *Swim with the Sharks Without Being Eaten Alive*, gives us his take on good management:

> *"Our goal is TGIM – Thank God it's Monday. We fight our guts out and use every bit of creativity that we can and manufacture as much fun as we can and we try to enhance all of our people's skills from the moment they are on the team. We try to do all of that so 100 percent of the 500 people that are coming to work on Monday are glad to be at work. Do we know that? Our best estimate is that 80 percent of the people can't wait to get to work."*

Dennis Madsen, CEO of Recreational Equipment, Inc., the largest consumer cooperative in the nation, was asked why his business was so successful. Here are a few of the things he said:

> *"People who work for REI have a genuine affection for the outdoors that goes beyond just making retail gear. The ideals we uphold every day to keep us on course are authenticity, quality, commitment to service, honesty, integrity, and just having fun. It isn't about the job. It's about nurturing a special spirit and culture that a great group of climbers had in their sights so many years ago."*

Madsen believes that the important elements of being a great leader include: dreaming big, putting together a winning team, never asking anyone to do something you wouldn't do yourself, and always putting on a game face no matter how bleak the situation might appear.

Caela Farren, CEO of MasteryWorks, gives us her view on what constitutes an effective manager:

> *"Managers who get to know their people, respect and trust the competency of their employees, and listen continually for how employees are doing relative to their aspirations, quality of work life, and a sense of career advancement, will have a far greater chance of developing and retaining their employees."*

The above are just a few examples of what great managers say we can do to keep our employees from quitting.

How Top Brass Fails Its Middle Managers

Why is there a lack of effective managers in our organizations today? I know from talking with thousands of workshop participants each year that there are a lot of good managers out there—but it seems there are more managers who don't know what they're doing than otherwise.

Why is this? Remember the statistic early in this book taken from a Harris Poll a few years ago? 85% of those in management positions have never had management training.

I place the onus for this right at the top: the CEO and upper management. It's amazing how many managers I talk to who were never given management training before being put in positions of authority over employees. I know of hundreds whose first experience of management training was when they attended one of my workshops. After years of working as managers!

How can we expect managers to know how to manage if they are not trained to do so? It's ludicrous to put an employee in charge of other employees' performance and behavior without first giving him the knowledge he needs to do it. PEOPLE ARE NOT BORN KNOWING HOW TO MANAGE!

One of the main mistakes companies make is putting their employees in management positions based on technical skills or years of service. Years of service and even high skills do not a manager make. Here's a word of advice for any HR considering putting someone in a management position: DO NOT PUT ANY PERSON IN A POSITION OF AUTHORITY UNLESS HE OR SHE HAS A REPUTATION FOR POSSESSING GOOD INTERPERSONAL SKILLS! Good people skills are #1 for motivating, retaining, gaining commitment, and getting quality performance and behavior from employees.

You may be wondering this: "I still haven't received any management training and I feel like I'm barely scraping by in my management abilities. What should I do?" First, take heart. You're reading this book, which is giving you the main ingredients you need to be successful in management. But don't stop here. Read other books and attend management seminars. Attend in-house training provided by your HR (hopefully your HR does provide some management training!). If your company will not invest in your success, take responsibility for your own growth.

John From Nevada Learned the Right Way to Manage

A former Microsoft employee named John decided to fly solo by building his own high tech company. Things didn't go smoothly the first year or so. He would invest money in training only to have employees quit when offered big bucks from companies that can afford huge salaries. John didn't know what to do to motivate his employees to stay with him.

John quickly took control. He began attending management seminars and reading books on how to manage and lead people. He went to work implementing much of what he learned. He began making his company a fun place to work. He bought a refrigerator and stocked it with soda for his employees, free of charge. He bought a popcorn machine and made popcorn every day. John did other wild and crazy things to make work an enjoyable place. He did all he could to get his employees the most up-to-date resources to do their jobs. He praised his employees and showed them appreciation for staying with his company, despite being offered more money with big companies. He empowered his employees and got them involved in decision-making.

John told me his business went from near bankruptcy to profitability within a year. It was due to the fact that he cared for his people and made them feel they were part of something special—part of an awesome company they could grow with.

Be the best manager you can be. I know of many employees who stay with their companies because they respect their boss. I know of many who stay with their companies because the CEO and upper management create such a great environment to work in, their employees know that culture of caring will be hard to find elsewhere.

Create an Organization Where People Don't Want to Leave

I once asked a man if he would be willing to work for me if I gave him $1.00 more an hour. He said no. I offered $2.00 more an hour. He said no. I offered $5.00 more an hour. He still said no. When I asked him why I couldn't take him away from his current job, he said, "Money cannot replace the wonderful environment I get to work in now. I've worked for other companies and quit because of lousy management. I know how hard it is to find a place to work where one feels appreciated and is given the resources to do the job right. Thanks for the offer, but no thanks."

It is possible to create great places to work. We already witnessed how it's possible in a union setting. It is also possible in federal, state, and city government environments. It just takes good managers who are willing to work the systems to make things happen. It does not happen over night, just as creating a critical mass leader doesn't happen overnight. But with vision and persistence, we can become the bosses we need to be to get things done and get them done right.

Action Plan — Try This For Fun

Your Best and Worst Boss

Think of the worst boss you ever had. Write down 10 characteristics that made you want to quit your boss:

1. _____   6. _____

2. _____   7. _____

3. _____   8. _____

4. _____   9. _____

5. _____   10. _____

Now think of the best boss you ever had. Write down 10 characteristics that made this person so effective and great to work with:

1. _____   6. _____

2. _____   7. _____

3. _____   8. _____

4. _____   9. _____

5. _____   10. _____

Your challenge is to commit yourself to live the characteristics of your best boss, and not be like your worst boss.

Try this out. For the next 21 working days, before you walk into your department, say this to yourself:

"Today, I will be this person. I will be..."

Then, either out loud or in your mind, list 10 positive characteristics that you will commit yourself to living that day. For example,

"Today I will be this person. I will be
kind, courteous, genuine, firm, fair,
a good listener, caring, compassionate,
decisive, and solution-oriented."

You may find by Day 22 that your management behavior has become more effective.

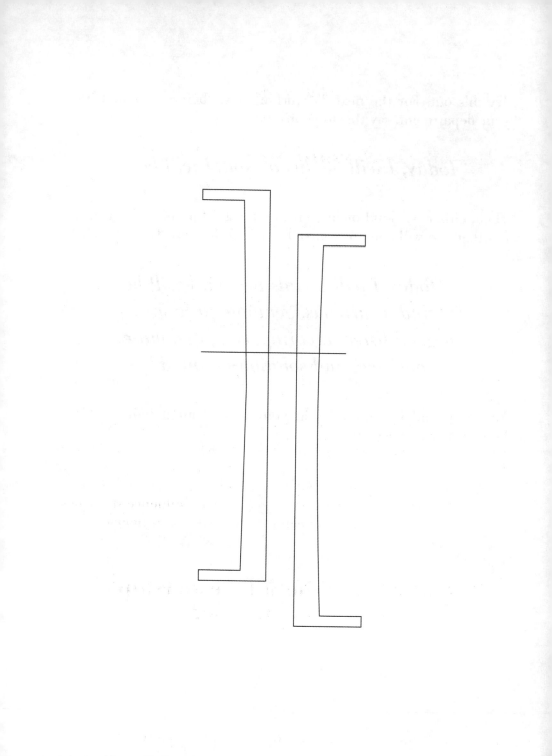

CHAPTER 11

The #1 Leadership Strategy of All Time

RESULTS! That's what management is all about. Results generate the bottom line. The way we obtain results is by using an arsenal of strategies to influence our employees toward the results we want.

This brings us to the topic of leadership. In order to get results we not only need to be exceptional managers, but also exceptional leaders. There is a huge difference between being a manager and a leader. Managers are problem solvers and take care of daily routines. Leaders, by contrast, are problem seekers. They motivate and inspire employees toward excellence and influence others toward a common vision.

One of our primary objectives should be this: to be exceptional managers AND leaders.

Effective leaders use various influence strategies to help them get the best performance and behavior from their employees. In this chapter I'll give you some of the most powerful influence strategies you'll ever learn, so that you can get the results top management expects from you.

What is the #1 Leadership Strategy of all time?

TURN THE PAGE TO FIND OUT! ☞

The Number One Secrets of Successful Managers

The #1 Leadership Strategy of All Time Is...

The Law of Reciprocity

Make the Rule of Reciprocity Work for You

In his book, *Influence: Science and Practice*, Robert Cialdini tells us that the rule of reciprocation is one of the most potent weapons of influence around us. Human culture has developed a system of indebtedness where people feel obligated to try to repay, in kind, what another person has provided. "If I scratch your back, you scratch mine."

Have you ever done a good turn for someone and when the time comes when you need help, you discover that person is more than willing to come to your aid? Or someone does you a good turn, and when they later ask for help you feel somewhat guilty if you can't return the favor? That is the law of reciprocity at work. It's implanted in all of us through thousands of years of socialization.

Leaders use actions and words to influence others to demonstrate a desired behavior, or to move toward a common vision. If we are to be leaders in our organizations, we need to learn the words and actions that will influence others toward peak performance.

Practical Ways to Use the Law of Reciprocity

Here are some practical ways we can use this #1 leadership strategy:

• DO FAVORS FOR PEOPLE IN YOUR ORGANIZATION.

When employees or colleagues ask for your help, make the time to accommodate them (without compromising other standards). In the future, they will feel obligated to return the favor when it's your turn to ask.

A training manager made time to help a manager in a systems department of his organization. The day came when the training manager needed help with a computer problem. He called the systems manager and asked for help. Within minutes a technician was in his office fixing the problem. The man called the systems manager and said, "Thank you for the immediate help you gave. I thought I'd have to sit on a list." The systems manager said, "No problem. I appreciate so much the help you gave me a week ago. Any time you have a problem with your computers, just give me a call and I'll send someone up right away."

Go out of your way to help your employees. Stay late once in a while to give extra assistance. Be willing to spend your lunch break now and then coaching and mentoring. Invest time in your employee's success. By showing your willingness to go the extra mile, your employees will be willing to go the extra mile for you.

The law of reciprocity can have a profound affect on conformity within your department. Cialdini tells us that the social group will dislike a person who violates the reciprocity rule. This puts pressure on your unthankful employee, who will change his behavior quickly if he wants to be accepted by the group. There is power in peer pressure.

• SHOW EVERYONE RESPECT.

Respect is a powerful reciprocity strategy. When we show someone respect, it's hard for that person not to reciprocate with respect. Human beings are typically kind to those who have shown them kindness.

• MAKE CONCESSIONS.

People naturally feel obligated to make concessions to someone who has done the same for them. Negotiate with your employees and be willing to compromise. Your employees will remember your concessions and will be more inclined to do what you ask. A wonderful by-product of making concessions is that your employees will be apt to do even more than you ask simply because you were willing to make concessions to them.

Do you see how powerful reciprocation is? Your employees will feel a sense of loyalty to you because you are loyal to them.

Develop an Arsenal of Influence Strategies

Now that you've discovered the #1 leadership strategy of all time, here are a few other leadership strategies to get the best from your employees:

- THE "EVERYONE ELSE IS DOING IT" STRATEGY

This is an influence tactic you will want to use ethically. Don't say, "Everyone else is doing it," if not everyone else is doing it. However, there is power in social proof. For example, if you want to move your department toward working as a team and you have one person who is hanging back, you may want to employ the strategy like this: "Bob, everyone in the department is committed to developing a team atmosphere and we'd like you to be part of it. If we can all work together, great things will happen." Because everyone else is doing it, Bob will be more inclined to change his attitude.

Advertisers use this strategy on us all the time. "Eight out of ten people use our product" or "Thirty million people who invest in our company can't be wrong." There's power in social proof.

- THE "YOU'RE GUILTY" STRATEGY

There's nothing wrong in making an employee feel guilty or selfish for not complying with the rules and norms of the department. For instance: "Bill, lately you've been abrasive with your coworkers and, as you know, we require that all employees behave with professional attitudes. The way you treated Janet in front of her coworkers was not professional. Come on in the office and let's talk."

- THE WIIFM STRATEGY

WIIFM is What's In It For Me. When we can show our employees the benefits of certain behavior or performance, commitment will follow.

Explaining the benefits of an action is one of the cornerstones of commitment and influence.

I remember the day in 1977 when I was thinking of joining the military. I was hesitant with my recruiter until he started pointing out the benefits. Much of my college tuition would be paid for. I would see different parts of the world. I'd always have a paycheck, even if I broke my leg and couldn't work for a month. And I'd be doing something great by defending my country. At that time in my life, I had no clear direction and my wife was pregnant. The benefits sold me.

In her book, *Power Phrases*, Meryl Runion gives us some practical benefit phrases to gain employee commitment when delegating:

> *"What this project means to you is…"*
>
> *"This will help you by…"*
>
> *"If you do this for me, I will…"*
>
> *"I'll make sure my boss knows how you made a difference when I really needed you."*
>
> *"You have shared with me how you want to excel in this company and climb the promotional ladder quickly. Here's a project that will get you visibility among the top brass."*

Get in the habit of showing your employees the benefits. Exceptional politicians, salespeople, trainers, religious leaders, business people, and managers have all learned this influence strategy.

"You can lead a horse to water, but you can't make it drink." This old adage reminds us that we can show another the road to change, but we cannot make him change. People have to be willing to change themselves. Let's turn that old adage into a leadership strategy:

> *"You can lead a horse to water,*
> *but you can't make it drink.*
> *But you sure can feed it salt tablets."*

Excellent leaders make their employees so thirsty they will want to drink the water. The best salt tablets are the salt tablets of benefit and value. Make your employees thirsty by showing them how change will benefit them. Show them what's in it for them. Show them how good performance and behavior will reflect on their employee evaluations, or help them build careers in the organization, or help them get that bonus or raise they've been seeking. The more benefits you can point out, the better.

• THE CREDIBILITY STRATEGY

The key to successful influence as leaders is credibility. Our influence strategies will succeed or fail dependent on how others perceive us. The Greek philosopher, Aristotle, taught a concept called ethos — source credibility — meaning that a speaker's persuasive power is largely dependent on how credible the audience thinks the speaker is.

Your employees evaluate your credibility every day. You are constantly under their microscopes. Here are some elements of credibility that will influence your employees and get the results you desire:

- *Competence.* Know and do your job well. Provide your employees the training they need to do their jobs well. Show your employees that you know what you're doing and what you're talking about. You'll lose credibility quickly if employees think you don't know what you're doing.

- *Honesty.* Employees will follow those they can trust. A recent survey asked employees the most important trait they look for in their bosses. Honesty was #1. Build trust with your employees by keeping your word.

- *Confidence.* Effective leaders exude confidence. Confident leaders stand for their beliefs and are not easily sidetracked from what they want to accomplish. Confident leaders are proactive and persistent.

• THE POSITIONAL POWER STRATEGY

Managers are lords of the manor. They have the power to reward and punish. Positional power resides in the position rather than in the person.

It's important to realize the power you have over your employees. You do not ever want to abuse this power. You also do not want to allow employees to be insubordinate. Reminding an employee that you are the boss comes in handy when attempting to correct mis-behavior or poor performance. With most employees, you'll rarely have to use your positional power. If you follow the management and leadership strategies outlined in this book, you will command the respect of most of your employees.

Where does power come from? Power is granted to a person by others. People make leaders. Leaders don't make themselves leaders. I can be given power from above to reward and punish, but if someone doesn't respect me, ultimately I don't have power over that person.

That's why we want to command respect, not demand it. We want employees to follow our lead because we're setting examples of excellence.

I once asked a group of people in a workshop to tell me what their bosses were like. Some said they did their jobs strictly out of fear of reprisal. These employees had no respect for their managers. A man then raised his hand and said, "Let me tell you about a boss I once had years ago. He was the best boss I ever had, and probably ever will have. His name was Colin Powell and he was my boss during the Gulf War. I would have gone to the ends of the earth for that man, as would the other soldiers under his command. He demanded a lot from us and also from himself. He commanded our respect. He practiced what he preached and walked the walk."

The best way to use your power, as we learned in Chapter 5, is to give it away. Empower your employees to get you the results you need. Use your power wisely.

Action Plan – Take the Influence Test

Have you learned the art of influence yet?

Take the influence test below and discover the areas where you're already doing well, as well as the areas where you can do better.

1 = poor; 3 = satisfactory; 5 = very good

1. I do favors for people to establish the reciprocity rule.

2. I show others respect to gain respect in return.

3. I make concessions now to gain commitment later.

4. I use the internal consistency strategy to facilitate change.

5. I use the social proof strategy to gain compliance.

6. If an employee isn't following the rules, I let him know it.

7. I point out WIIFM benefits to gain commitment.

8. I am competent in my job to demonstrate credibility.

9. I am trustworthy.

10. I am confident in my ability as a leader.

11. I know I am lord of the manor and I use my power wisely.

12. I command the respect of my employees. I don't demand it.

How did you do? If you answered any questions with a 1 or 3, come up with an action plan to improve in that area. If you rated yourself a 5 in any area, keep up the good work in influencing your employees toward peak performance.

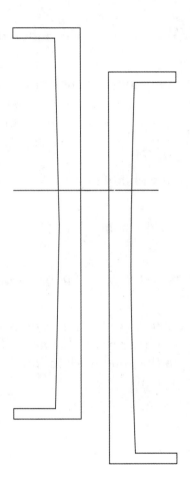

CHAPTER 12

The #1 Quality Every Leader Must Have

There's one quality that every leader must have to be regarded as a leader. Martin Luther King, Jr. had it. Ghandi had it. Napoleon had it. Queen Elizabeth has it. Emperor Constantine had it. Even Adolph Hitler had it. If we are to be leaders in our organizations, we must have this #1 quality too. We can lack compassion, but if we have this quality we will still be regarded as leaders. We can even lack integrity, but if we have this quality we will still be regarded as leaders.

What is the #1 quality every person must have to be considered a leader?

TURN THE PAGE TO FIND OUT! ☞

The Number One Secrets of Successful Managers

The #1 Quality Every Leader Must Have Is...

Visionary People Make Things Happen

Every leader has vision. Every leader has something in mind he or she wants to accomplish in the future. According to Hackman and Johnson in their book, *Leadership: A Communication Perspective*, effective leaders create a desirable vision for what the group or organization should be in the future.

Effective leaders are adept at selecting and articulating vision. Effective leaders have the ability, through the use of influence strategies, to energize others toward a common vision. An effective leader knows that employees don't commit to vision through edicts or decrees, but because it's right for employees and the organization.

Leaders are on a crusade in life. Martin Luther King, Jr. had a vision for tolerance. Ghandi had a vision for an India free from British rule. Marriott Hotels has the vision of being the #1 hotel chain in the world. It's up to managers to align their employees to the vision of their organizations. When employees aren't aligned and energized about the corporate vision, they tend to lose their allegiance. Without a vision, work is more about the paycheck than being a vital part of building something great.

Leadership Is More Than a Paycheck

Three men were working on a wall. A woman walking by asked the first man, "What are you doing?" The man said, "I'm making a paycheck."

The woman asked the second man, "What are you doing?" The man said, "I'm just doing what I'm told. I'm building a wall."

The woman approached the third man. "Sir, what are you doing?"

The third man smiled and said with a sparkle in his eyes, "I'm building a cathedral where someday men and women will come to worship."

That third man had vision. He believed he was part of something great. He wasn't there just to make a paycheck or simply to get the job done. He was there to build a cathedral.

The most effective managers are leaders too. These manager/leaders know how to inspire their employees to share the company vision. They know which strategies to use to influence their employees to take on the crusade. They believe that work is more than a paycheck or getting the work done. They're on a mission to build a fantastic organization that will be successful in reaching its vision.

Make Sure You Are Part of the Program

Managers must believe in their organization's mission and vision. It's a must to be an effective leader. Managers are partners with the CEO in making the company vision become a reality.

I once conducted training in a company that made video slot machines. One manager said, "I can't buy into the mission and vision of this organization. We make a product that soaks the elderly of their social security checks, and gets some people addicted to gambling. How do you expect me to share the vision of a company like that?"

I looked him in the eye and said, "The best thing for you to do is to head to your HR department because you need to quit right now. If you can't accept the vision of this company, you can't be an effective manager."

The man was shocked, but I was there to train managers to be the glue of their organizations. During lunch, I talked with the man and he disclosed that he's a strong Christian who has a moral problem with gambling. I told him that either he needed to look for another job or find a way to reconcile his beliefs with the product and the company vision.

Are you energizing your employees to be excited about the vision of your company?

Charge the Competition

The 1989 film *Glory* is a shining example of what it means to have vision and get others committed to that vision. Matthew Broderick plays Colonel Robert Shaw, a young officer responsible for training one of the first black regiments during the Civil War. Colonel Shaw was a leader. He instilled in his men a sense of destiny, a sense of vision.

The test of his leadership comes at the end of the movie, when Shaw and his men charge the impenetrable Fort Wagner. It's a suicide run. Flares light the night sky. Cannon balls shatter the ground. Bullets rain from above. After hours of being pinned down, Colonel Shaw decides it's time to make their last stand. With the American flag in one hand and a pistol in the other, Shaw stands and yells for his men to storm the fort. Three paces into the charge Shaw is gunned down and killed. But his spirit and vision live on in his men. Right behind Colonel Shaw is a soldier played by Denzel Washington. He stoops down amidst the clamor of war, picks up the American flag from his beloved leader's limp hand and leads the charge forward. Seconds later, he is also gunned down and killed.

By this time, you'd think the rest of the men would have received a reality check and hightailed it out of there. But not these men! They were on a crusade for freedom. They believed in and were energized by their vision. Behind Denzel Washington is another soldier — his glasses broken, bloody face, mud caked all over his body. With one courageous swoop, he grabs the American flag from the dead hand of his friend and charges the fort.

Charge your competition. Don't settle for the mundane or mediocre. Be a leader and make things happen. Build that cathedral, where employees can enjoy a culture of praise and empowerment. Know what you stand for and be persistent. Not everyone will appreciate your proactive attitude — whiners and complainers can't stand positive people. Remember, you weren't hired to be anyone's friend. You were hired to accord everyone the same respect and dignity you expect for yourself. You were hired to create leaders who will seize the organizational vision and get the job done.

Action Plan

What Is Your Vision?

Write down a vision you have for your life. Next, write down three things you're doing to make your vision happen.

Write down your vision for your department. What do you want it to be like in the future? Write down three actions you're taking to make things happen in your department.

Write down your organization's vision and mission statements. If you don't know them, why not? Does upper management expect all employees to know the organization's mission and vision statements? If not, they should. All employees should be aligned to the mission and vision of the organization. Take a look at your organization's mission and vision statements. If each is longer than one sentence, they're too long. If you don't have them, then what are your employees working toward?

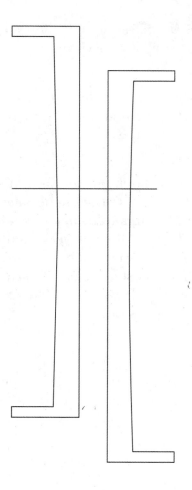

CHAPTER 13

The #1 Way to Lead

Many management and leadership books talk about three styles of leadership: autocratic, democratic, and laissez-faire (or indirect) leadership.

These three leadership styles, identified and researched in the late 1930s, are still taught today in many colleges and leadership workshops.

Autocratic leaders TELL people what to do. The leader makes all decisions and followers are expected to comply. It's the "my way or the highway" style of leadership. Democratic leaders ASK people what to do. People are encouraged to participate in decision-making and are empowered to carry out the task or project. Indirect leaders play golf while their followers get things done. Very little supervision is needed to get results.

Which leadership style do you think is the best? I like the idea of being an autocratic leader. If employees don't like my decisions, they can quit and go somewhere else.

Wait! I've changed my mind. Maybe I like democratic leadership more. Ask employees for their suggestions and listen to their concerns.

Wait! I've changed my mind again. I really like the idea of playing golf and trusting my employees to do the jobs they were hired to do.

What do you think? Which leadership style is the best—autocratic, democratic, or indirect?

What is the #1 way to lead?

TURN THE PAGE TO FIND OUT! ☞

The Number One Secrets of Successful Managers

The #1 Way to Lead Is...

According to the Situation

Using All Three Is the Key to Successful Leadership

There is no number one way to lead. The best leaders use all three leadership styles at different times according to the situation, the task, and the employee. This is called Situational Leadership. Ken Blanchard, author of the best-selling book, *The One-Minute Manager*, developed this approach to leadership in the 1970s. It is still one of the most popular leadership theories today.

Situational leadership takes into account both the situation and the maturity level of the employee. The leader then picks the leadership style that will reap the best results and benefit the employee and the organization the most. It is the leader who changes his or her behavior, not the employee. Remember, we can't change anyone. But we can use certain influence tactics to make the employee thirsty for change.

All three leadership styles are viable and useful in getting the results we desire. There are times we will tell employees what to do; there are times we'll ask employees what they think and empower them; and there are times we'll keep our hands off and allow employees to make decisions without any direct influence from us.

Work Yourself Out of a Job Through Situational Leadership

As a manager, do you remember your #1 goal? If not, turn to Chapter 4 and refresh your memory. We learned that the theory of critical mass and empowering employees through proper delegation are two of the most powerful ways of accomplishing this.

Using situational leadership properly is another way of reaching our #1 goal—that is, to work ourselves out of a job. If we can get the majority of our employees to the place where we can employ indirect leadership most of the time, we will not be needed by them very often. Not being needed by our employees is a great place to be.

Let me take you step-by-step through the process of making this happen.

When a new employee is going through orientation, use autocratic leadership. You will tell them what to do because new employees want to be told what to do. They're nervous about the job and don't know everything they need to know. They're unsure of the people they'll be working with and need constant direction.

As the orientation proceeds, begin investing in the employee's "Emotional Bank Account" as Stephen Covey tells us to do. Build your credibility by showing the employee you care about his or her success. Make the employee feel valued. Praise and show appreciation. Listen when there are questions. Manage by Wandering Around to give and get consistent feedback about the employee's performance.

Once the orientation is complete and you know you can trust that employee to do the job he or she was hired to do, segue from telling leadership to asking, democratic leadership. As the employee's task and behavioral maturity grows, begin delegating to and empowering the employee. Ask for the employee's input on decisions and listen to suggestions. Challenge the employee to be solution-oriented and proactive in helping the department and organization reach its mission and vision. Gain commitment through involvement. Continue to show the benefits of being part of the team. As always, Manage by Wandering Around so you are always aware of how your employee is doing.

Once you have that employee mostly in a democratic mode, move toward indirect leadership. Empower the employee to make his or her own decisions. Give the employee ownership over tasks and projects, and hold the employee accountable for results. Mentor the employee on becoming a critical mass leader. Allow the employee to make mistakes without fear of reprisal. As time goes by, pull away from the employee and give very little direction or supervision. Allow the employee to begin calling his or her own shots on how to manage the job. Trust yourself that you have been successful in creating an employee who rarely needs you anymore.

If you can get 70 to 80 percent of your people to be indirect leadership employees, you are doing a fantastic job and will have a smooth running department.

Your Greatest Challenge as a Manager and Leader

Your greatest challenge as a manager and leader is to get your employees working as a cohesive team, so they can be self-directed and take ownership over the running of the department.

Can it be done? Absolutely! Does it happen overnight? Absolutely not!

To grow an employee from initial orientation to using indirect leadership can take years of coaching and mentoring. It will take all kinds of influence salt tablets to facilitate the behavioral changes you desire.

This is all dependent on the maturity and skill of each employee. Some employees are innately proactive and show passion and enthusiasm for their work. After orientation they need little supervision. Other employees may be more self-centered. They're in it only for the paycheck and do not care about the mission and vision of the organization. These employees will need more coaching and mentoring, and sometimes a firm hand to get them working well with others.

Even when your team is mostly self-directed, you will continue to use situational leadership. At times, such as in an emergency situation that calls for an immediate response, you will have to make a quick decision and use autocratic leadership, regardless of what your employees have to say. Even your best proactive employees will slip up once in a while. On these occasions, you may have to exert a more autocratic manner to obtain the results you desire.

Don't Get Stuck in a Rut

One of the dangers of leadership is to get stuck using only one style of leadership at all times. Autocratic managers who are stuck in the rut of making all the decisions and always telling employees what to do are doomed to failure. These are the dinosaur managers who are still living in medieval times. Democratic managers who are always asking for input and getting employees involved in decision making may find it hard to make unpopular decisions. Employees who sometimes need a manager with decisive strokes may perceive this as wishy-washy. Indirect managers who are always "out of the office" will find themselves in a world of chaos when the CEO wants answers about why performance levels are dropping.

Be a situational leader. Be aware of the skill levels and maturity of each of your employees and lead accordingly. Don't be afraid to make unpopular decisions. Act decisively when you need to. Give power and authority to employees who desire to grow and be challenged. Remember, you want to work yourself out of a job.

Action Plan

Develop Your Employees into Indirect Leadership Employees

Write the names of all the employees whom you directly supervise. Next to each employee's name, write the style of leadership you tend to use most of the time with that person.

For example, you may have a few employees who are self-motivated, proactive, rarely need supervision, and can be trusted to do their jobs when you're away. Write "Indirect" next to their names. You may have a few employees who constantly need direction and only do what is required of them. They are not team players. Write "Autocratic" next to their names. You may have other employees who need direct supervision now and then, are team players, desire to be empowered, and can be trusted to do their jobs most of the time. Write "Democratic" next to their names.

Your challenge as a leader is this: to use your influence strategies to get as many of your employees as you can to require only indirect leadership most of the time.

Underneath each employee's name, write three strategies you can use to move your autocratic employees toward being more democratic, and your democratic employees toward being more indirect. Underneath your indirect employees, write down three ways you can get them involved in helping to grow your other employees into critical mass leaders.

Build a department full of leaders who take ownership for their jobs. This takes time and energy, so be persistent. If one strategy fails, use another.

Make each employee thirsty for leadership by showing them the benefits of being leaders, both in your department and the organization.

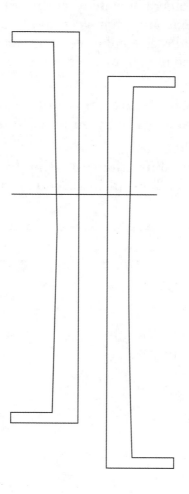

CHAPTER 14

The #1 Problem in Most Organizations

When I've asked thousands of managers and employees to share what they think is the #1 problem in their organizations, 90 percent say the same thing. This #1 problem is the major cause of poor results and substandard performance. It's the #1 reason employees have bad attitudes towards management and managers have poor attitudes towards employees. It's also one of the most easily fixed problems in any organization.

What do you think is the #1 problem in most organizations?

Take a guess. You're probably right! Your organization may be suffering from it right now.

TURN THE PAGE TO FIND OUT! ☞

The #1 Problem in Most Organizations Is...

A Lack of
Effective
Communication

A Lack of Effective Communication

Did you guess right? Most employees feel "out of the loop." They complain that management doesn't listen to them. They feel they are "in the dark" about decisions and changes that affect them directly. The #1 problem in most organizations is that people are not talking effectively to one another. Top brass is not talking effectively with their managers; managers aren't talking effectively with their employees; employees aren't talking effectively with their managers; managers aren't talking effectively with managers in other departments.

It's the "Effective" That's Missing, Not the Communication

Did you notice how the word "effectively" kept repeating in the above paragraph? When asked the question, "What do you think is the #1 problem in organizations today?" most say, "A lack of communication." But it's impossible to have a lack of communication in any organization. People communicate whether they want to or not. By not communicating, we are communicating. One of the main tenets of communication is:

We cannot NOT communicate.

It is the lack of EFFECTIVE communication that is the #1 problem in most organizations. For example, if I stay in my office all day and don't talk with my employees, I am communicating something to my employees. In their minds, I'm communicating that I don't care about their success. If I sit at my computer and continue typing while an employee is trying to talk with me, they will think I'm not listening.

Good Intentions Do Not Equal Good Communication

"But," you hasten to say, "I do communicate with my employees and they still don't get the message. My intentions are good." Just because you talk doesn't mean you're communicating effectively. And just because your intentions are good doesn't mean you're communicating effectively. This brings us to another main tenet of communication:

The meaning of communication is in the response of others, not in our intentions.

All the good intentions in the world don't mean that the listener is receiving the message the way you meant him to receive it. Effective communication occurs when the other person gets the meaning we intended. When we keep employees out of the loop, they think we don't care about them. We may not feel that way, but our feelings don't matter. It's what others are thinking and the meaning they assign to our actions and words that ultimately affect their performance and behavior toward the organization. How employees respond to our message IS the message, whether we intended that message or not.

Making the Grade Through Effective Communication

It is important for everyone in every organization to be taught effective communication skills, from the top brass down. Every HR department should afford all members of the organization the chance to attend either in-house communication training, or pay for them to attend communication workshops. Why is this so important? There is a direct correlation between effective communication and employee performance and job satisfaction. Here's what some of the experts have to say:

> "An organization needs to regularly communicate to enable employees to feel engaged, to feel valued, to seek their input, to keep them aware and to enable them to manage their jobs. The measurement of communication is key for organizational effectiveness and employee satisfaction. The circumstances and conditions that organizations face today create a sense of urgency that wasn't there before. If people don't feel engaged or connected with the organization they work for, they're going to go elsewhere."
>
> —BRAIN LOWENTHAL, DIRECTOR AT
> HACKETT BENCHMARKING & RESEARCH

> "Communication is even more critical as our organizations face these incredible staffing challenges. There are a lot of indications that employee communication programs can have a direct impact on recruiting, development, and retention, and I believe, productivity too."
>
> —NICK BURKHOLDER, VICE PRESIDENT
> AT BERNARD HODES GROUP

*Your organization's success is based on
how well its members communicate.*

Do You Make the Grade as an Effective Communicator?

Your success as a manager is also based on how well you communicate. Do you genuinely listen to your employees? Do you keep them in the loop and constantly share important information and skills? Do you consistently give and receive feedback from each employee?

Effective communication isn't just your words. It's your actions too.

"Actions speak louder than words."

–Your Grandma

"It's not what you say, but how you say it."

–Your Great Grandma

Effective managers are shining examples of what it means to be good communicators. They walk the talk.

Doing It Right

Tavern on the Green, the famed eatery in New York City, does it right when it comes to communication. They met the challenge of retaining good employees by improving communication between employees and management. Some of the communication strategies they've implemented:

- Open monthly forums in which employees can talk with managers about their suggestions and concerns.
- A quarterly newsletter that shares successes
- Thank you cards
- A suggestion box
- Treating employees as partners

Can you think of any other ways you can keep employees in the loop and keep the lines of communication open? How about trying these ideas:

- An e-mail address dedicated to uncovering the causes of turnover, as well as employee suggestions and concerns.
- Regular hours when your door is open for employees to talk.
- A five-minute team meeting each morning to ensure you and your employees are on the same page, and to give clear direction, if necessary.

Harvey MacKay, author of *Beware of the Naked Man Who Offers You His Shirt*, relates this story about the CEO of a company where he worked:

" Our president meets with every single employee for half an hour and asks, 'What's on your mind, what are your likes, what are your dislikes, and if you could change something, what would you change?' He then asks about their interest in continuing education and asks, 'What are your dreams?' All the while he takes copious notes, and he does this once a year. Isn't that beautiful?"

Now there's a CEO who knows the importance of keeping the lines of communication open.

I was in Albuquerque, New Mexico a year ago and asked a young woman behind the ticket counter at Southwest Airlines, "Do you know who your CEO is?" I didn't ask this question to embarrass her. As a management trainer, I like to hear from the mouths of employees what their CEOs are really like and not just read about them in books. She said, "Oh yes, his name is Herb Kelleher." I asked if she had ever met him, and she said, "It's funny you should ask. He was here just a few weeks ago and he was such a nice man. He came around the counter and talked to all of us. He asked us what we liked about the company and what we thought would make it even better."

I was impressed that the CEO of a Fortune 500 company was meeting with employees and soliciting their feedback. We can learn a lot about communication from the likes of Herb Kelleher.

Try These Communication Tips

Here are a few more tips to guide you on your journey:

- Communicate to BUILD UP, NOT TEAR DOWN. What comes out of your mouth should edify, not destroy. One word spoken in anger or hate can devastate your relationship with an employee FOREVER. Keep in mind another thing grandma has been teaching us for centuries:

"If you don't have anything good to say,
don't say it."

- Ask questions to clarify information. Asking questions is the most powerful communication tool we have at our disposal. We want to ask specific, precise questions to ensure that the person has received the message we intended, or to ensure we understand the person's intended message. Questions such as:

- "What specifically is it about this task you don't understand?"
- "What exactly am I doing wrong in my performance?"
- "This is how I see the problem. How do you see it?"
- "I have a hard time believing that no one in this organization listens to you. Who exactly do you feel doesn't listen to you?"
- "Why did you think you had the right to go over my head without consulting with me first?"
- "Can you give me some specific examples of how you think we can do things better?"
- "Hi Bob. Tell me how things are going for you in our department."
- "Susan, I want to make sure I'm hearing what you are saying. What I'm getting out of your comments so far is…"
- "Joe, was that comment you just made meant to belittle me? I'm sure you didn't mean to embarrass me in front of my employees."

Get in the habit of asking questions even if you think you understand what the person is saying. Don't go too overboard with this or you'll drive people crazy always asking questions. Be tactful, discreet, and seek to understand.

- Listen. When someone is talking to you, stop what you're doing and give that person your full attention. Make eye contact. Ask questions if you are unsure of what the person is trying to say. Show the person you are interested in what they're saying, even if you're not. Just because something isn't important to you doesn't mean it isn't important to them.

By really listening, you build your investment in that person's emotional bank account.

Be the Best Communicator You Can Be

Read books and listen to tapes about effective communication. Go to workshops, and start communication training in your own department. Keep the lines of communication open. Share your skills and don't hoard information. Ask your employees, "What's on your mind?" Solicit feedback. Listen to your employees. MANAGE BY WANDERING AROUND!

What's In It For You? Promotions. Raises. Respect from superiors, peers, and subordinates. The ability to communicate well is ranked the #1 key to success in business, politics, and the professions. Learn to be an EFFECTIVE communicator. Your management experience will be much better for it.

Action Plan–Reality Check

Are you perceived as an effective communicator?

Set up an informal meeting with five people in your organization — employees you trust, your peers from other departments, and your own boss (if you feel comfortable with that). Ask them to discuss with you the following questions:

- Do you think I am perceived as an effective communicator in my department?
- Do I listen well when others talk with me? What can I work on?
- Am I perceived as a caring person or an abrasive person? What can I work on?
- Do I keep employees in our department in the loop? What can we do to increase communication in our department?
- What can I do to be perceived as an even better communicator?
- What are the things I'm doing right so I can continue doing those things?

Ideally you will get honest answers. Only ask those you trust who want to help you grow. You may be surprised at their answers. You may need to grow in areas you thought you were doing well in. You may be perceived as an effective communicator in areas where you were being too hard on yourself.

CHAPTER 15

The #1 Way to Reduce Stress in the Workplace

Feeling stressed out at work? Are you doing too much work and don't have enough employees to delegate to? Do you go home tired, not looking forward to work the next day?

There is a way to eliminate much of the stress in your life and your department. The #1 way is not deep breathing, even though deep breathing does wonders in relieving stress. The #1 way is not exercise, even though exercise is also great at reducing stress. The #1 way is not going into the bathroom and screaming your guts out, even though private moments of letting it all out can help you unburden your stressors. If none of the above,

What then is the #1 way to reduce stress in the workplace?

TURN THE PAGE TO FIND OUT! ☞

The Number One Secrets of Successful Managers

The #1 Way to Reduce Stress in the Workplace Is...

Teamwork

That's it! Teamwork. There's no better way to reduce stress than people helping each other to succeed. We need each other to make it through life, and to make good things happen in our organizations.

Some organizations do not practice teamwork. When I'm invited into many organizations to teach management and leadership skills, many times the human resources department will ask me to cover teamwork. They usually mention a significant lack of cooperation between workers and departments, severe enough to affect morale and performance.

Do You Believe in Teamwork?

When asked this question, the participants in my seminars always give a resounding, "YES!" Then I give them an exercise. I tell them they only have three minutes to live, and the only way to survive is to complete the following task within three minutes.

Connect all nine dots using only four straight lines.

Rules: Once you put your pen down, you can not lift it up. You can not retrace any line, but can cross any line. Go!

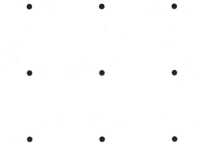

(Turn to end of this chapter to discover how to complete the exercise.)

The clock starts ticking. Every thirty seconds, I ask those who know how to complete the exercise to raise their hand. Usually by the end of three minutes, 25 percent of the group completes the task. During those three minutes, some participants work feverishly to complete the exercise, while others quit in frustration. When the clock stops, the majority of the room has not completed the task.

I then ask the same question I asked before the exercise. "Do you believe in teamwork?" Again they say yes. I ask, "Are you sure you believe in teamwork? If so, no one in this room would have died. Those who knew how to complete the task would have been helping others, and those who didn't know how to complete the task would have been asking for help." Usually there are moans and groans and shaking of heads. I ask, "Why did you allow your teammates to die?"

Participants give me many answers. "I don't know the person next to me well enough." Or, "You didn't tell us we could work together." Or, "I wanted to see if I could do it on my own."

Granted, participants didn't know one another and did not have the chance to grow together as a team, but there is still a lesson to be learned: If they had helped each other, all would have succeeded.

It never happens that everyone survives this exercise. It came pretty close once in Colorado Springs. When the clock started, immediately two people knew how to do it. They both stood up and shouted, "Does anyone need help? We know how to do it." People began calling for help and the two women went into action. Within a minute, once they learned how to complete the exercise, other participants began offering help. There was laughter and excitement in the air. But there was one table that refused help. A woman asked one of the men at that table if he needed help and the man said, "No thanks. We can do it on our own." Everyone completed the task except the one table that refused to ask for or accept help.

The Benefits of Teamwork

You can influence your employees to buy into teamwork by using the WIIFM strategy—show them "What's In It For Me" and the organization.

- **Reduced Stress.** When people work together, stress is greatly reduced. We stop feeling alone. The overwhelming frustration that can come with too much work is reduced when we tackle the work together. There's nothing more powerful than a group of people working together.

Did you know that the two most commonly prescribed drugs in the United States are Prozac and Valium? Did you know that Americans work longer hours than any other nation in the world? Did you know that many countries, such as Australia, give their employees a month's paid vacation every year? Did you know that the majority of lost hours at work are due to stress-related illnesses and issues?

If you are stressed at work, ask yourself how much your department is working together as a team. Are employees helping other employees when their work is done? Are many projects and tasks a team effort, instead of employees working on their own? If not, it's time to start building your group into a cohesive team—before they burn out or stress out by being asked to do more for less.

- **Increased Morale.** Teamwork increases morale and establishes esprit de corps. When people work together, there's an energy unequalled in human experience. Many workshop participants tell me they have fun and look forward to going to work because everyone works together.

While in the Air Force, to hone my medical skills and learn how to respond during war or disaster, I was required once a year to attend a two-day medical exercise. The first year I grumbled the entire time. I had to eat food out of pouches that tasted like wood, set up huge back-breaking tents, stay up 20 hours a day, and go the whole time without a shower. I was miserable.

The second year I had the same attitude. I whined and complained about everything. A sergeant overheard me complaining and said,

"Hal, it's up to you how this experience is going to be. You can either complain and get a reputation as a whiner, or you can get your behind in gear, be part of the team, and make it fun."

I decided to be part of the team and make it fun. By doing so, my perception of the experience changed. I had fun laughing and joking while putting up those huge tents. I had fun tossing some of the hard crackers at my team members. I had fun trudging across the mock battlefield as I carried a litter with three other team members.

It is possible to have fun at work. And the best way to have fun is to do it with a team.

- **Increased Performance.** Two hands are better than one. And three hands are better than two. When people work together, more gets done—many times with better results. When people work together, they don't tire as quickly and they can do more in less time.

- **Decreased Work Hours.** Did you know that work expands to fill the time allotted to it? If you allot 12 hours to work every day, you'll spend 12 hours doing the job. In fact, studies show that overtime equates to lost productivity because employees are tired and not mentally sharp every day. They spend more time taking breaks, drinking coffee, and doing non-vital activities to try to recharge their physiological batteries. The main culprit being this: some management fails to develop cohesive teams in their organizations. Some managers are too busy defending their turf and creating their own kingdoms to spend time making smart decisions with the team…to discover ways of working smarter, not harder.

- **Increased Flexibility.** More and more companies are learning the importance of cross-training employees to know more than one job. One of the main benefits of this is increased flexibility. Employees can help each other and even cover for one another because they're skilled in more than one area. There's nothing worse than having an employee call in sick when no one knows that person's job.

Teamwork will help eliminate that problem. A team environment allows employees to take ownership over time. For example, if Larry wants to take an extra hour for lunch to watch his son in a school play, no problem. Joyce will cover for him. When Joyce wants to take off an hour early to watch her daughter in a tennis tournament, no problem. Larry will cover for her. Teamwork affords this type of flexibility.

A manager in New Mexico empowered his team to make a radical schedule change. When he asked his team what could be done to increase morale, they suggested that they be allowed to make their own schedules—as long as they put in their 40 hours, got the work done, and continued to delight customers. The manager asked his boss for permission to try out this radical new schedule for one month to see if it would improve performance and morale. The boss gave the thumbs up.

Within a few weeks, the empowered employees were creating their own schedules. One employee worked twelve-hour days and took three-day weekends. Another employee worked twelve hours one day, two hours the next, fourteen hours the third day, three hours the fourth day, and nine hours the day after that. Others worked similar hours.

Within one month, employee morale and performance skyrocketed. The employees knew the guidelines and standards that had to be met, and they helped each other exceed the standards. They wanted this new way of scheduling to work, and knew it was in their hands to make it happen. They were empowered to take charge of their own destinies.

The manager's boss gave the go-ahead to allow these employees to continue making their own schedules. The manager said his department became so successful and team-oriented that other employees were begging to come work for him. Word spread about his success and months later he was lauded in front of his peers for innovative thinking.

The High Cost of Not Working Together as a Team

Teamwork works.
Not working together is costly.

An 18-year-old male came to an emergency room believing he had the flu. He was sent home after being examined by a doctor. The next day he came in by ambulance with meningitis, and died six hours later. Afterward, a nurse said she'd suspected meningitis the first time the young man came in. She didn't say anything because a doctor had scolded her two weeks earlier for speaking up about another patient. He said to her, "I'm the doctor, you stick to nursing."

Lack of teamwork cost that young man his life. A lack of teamwork in our organizations may not cost someone his life, but it's costly just the same in the time, money, and performance it takes to rectify problems due to lack of teamwork. Many great companies such as Toyota, Marriott Hotels, MCI, Xerox, Wal-Mart, and Federal Express have adopted the philosophy of teamwork, with awesome results.

Wal-Mart Does It Right

A young woman I passed in Wal-Mart said, "Sir, welcome to Wal-Mart. If there's anything I can do to assist you, just ask." I told her I was looking for duct tape and she directed me to Hardware. I passed two employees who were stocking shelves. One said to the other, "When I'm done, I'll help you." I was impressed. A young man noticed I was searching the shelves and said, "Sir, can I help you find something?" He stopped what he was doing and took me directly to the duct tape. As I was walking away, I overheard him say to another, "I'm not doing anything right now. Let me help you stock the shelves."

Where does that type of team attitude come from? Right from the top. For teamwork to be alive and well in an organization, the CEO and upper management must believe in it and make it happen. Teamwork should be one of the core values of every organization. In a team environment, you rarely hear this: "That's not in my job description." It's a sad day when an employee doesn't want to help a fellow teammate.

Living Teamwork

A man was sitting in the bleachers one day, videotaping the Special Olympics. Excitement filled the air. The crowd was cheering and clapping for the young participants with Down's Syndrome. The time came for the 50-yard dash and a group of teenagers walked to the starting line. The gun went off and the crowd went wild. The man in the bleachers followed the leaders with his camera. It was so noisy you couldn't hear the person sitting next to you.

Then something strange happened. The runners in the lead stopped in their tracks and turned backwards. More of the runners stopped and turned around. The cameraman was puzzled, so he zoomed out with his camera lens to get a better view of the whole field. There, struggling to get up, was a young man who had fallen at the starting line.

The crowd went silent. You could hear a pin drop. The runners turned and ran back down the field. They gathered around their fallen comrade and picked him up in their arms. Then, amidst the cheers of the crowd, they carried their teammate down the field and crossed the finish line together.

If you want some shining examples of teamwork, watch the Special Olympics, or walk through Wal-Mart, or fly Southwest Airlines. You'll find people who make it their business to help each other and work together as a team.

Action Plan

Get Your Department Working Together as a Team

Rate your department on each of the following:
1 = poor,   3 = satisfactory,   5 = excellent

1. Employees have been coached to think
of themselves as a team 1   3   5

2. Employees are held accountable for morale 1   3   5

3. Employees feel ownership for their jobs 1   3   5

4. Employees are cross-trained to learn other jobs 1   3   5

5. Flexibility is the norm due to teamwork 1   3   5

6. Due to teamwork we have minimal stress 1   3   5

7. We have high morale due to teamwork 1   3   5

8. Employees make most of the decisions 1   3   5

9. Employees go out of their way to help each other 1   3   5

10. Overtime is kept to a minimum due to teamwork 1   3   5

Did you rate any area with a 1 or 3? If so, come up with an action plan to work toward a 5 in each area.

Answer to Exercise

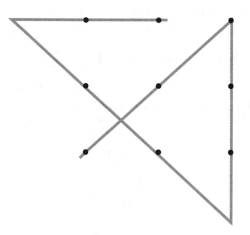

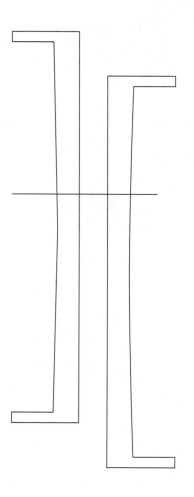

CHAPTER 16

The #1 Reason for
Poor Performance or Behavior

Imagine this: You're driving down the road and a police officer pulls you over. The officer gives you a stern look. "You were going too fast."

You look back at the officer, puzzled. You don't think you were going too fast. "How fast was I going?"

"I'm not sure," replies the officer, "but you were going too fast."

"But surely, officer, you must know how fast I was going. To tell you the truth, I don't remember ever seeing a speed sign in your state."

"We don't have speed signs. But by my estimation, you were going too fast."

Now you're really questioning things. "Well, how fast is too fast?"

"Don't get smart with me," says the officer. "Too fast is too fast, so I'm giving you a ticket."

Your frustration builds. "How can you give me a ticket for a law I haven't broken?" The officer shakes his head and says, "We don't have laws in this state. We're all adults here. We should know how fast is too fast and you were going too fast." The officer hands you a ticket and drives away.

Is there something wrong with this picture? Unfortunately, this type of scenario is happening in many organizations today. And it's the #1 reason for poor performance and behavior.

What is the #1 reason for
poor performance or behavior?

TURN THE PAGE TO FIND OUT! ☞

The Number One Secrets of Successful Managers

The #1 Reason for Poor Performance or Behavior Is...

A Lack of Measurable Standards

#1 Reason for Poor Performance or Behavior is A Lack of Measurable Standards

What's wrong with the picture is that the police officer was lacking ways to help you assess the situation. He didn't have anything to measure your speed against, so he based his judgment on purely subjective criteria.

Can you image the United States without the Constitution? Can you imagine a nation without laws to govern the behavior of its citizens? Can you imagine a family environment where the parents have no rules for their children? Without laws and rules, society falls into anarchy.

Stop Organizational Anarchy Through Measurable Standards

Unfortunately, some organizations have fallen into anarchy. Employees are allowed to under-perform and misbehave. The #1 reason for this is due to a lack of measurable standards — standards employees are expected to adhere to and managers expected to uphold.

Brian Tracey, one of America's premier management and business trainers, makes this statement in many of his books:

*"If it can't be measured,
it can't be managed."*

Organizations that lack measurable standards are in for a bumpy ride. Even though the subjective side of management will always be present, management should be more objective. Managers must have standards by which to govern performance and behavior — standards that establish what is and is not good performance and behavior.

What Every Organization Must Have to Run Smoothly

To better understand what every business—from the mom and pop furniture store to Xerox—must have in order to run smoothly, let's take a look at a fast food restaurant called Hamburger Haven. It's a small town place frequented by locals. Here are the standards Hamburger Haven has implemented to better measure employee performance and behavior. As you read, consider whether or not your organization has these standards on board to help managers manage and employees perform.

Mission Statement

Every organization must have a mission statement. Mission statements tell employees the purpose of the organization. All personnel should be required to know it. This brings managers and employees into alignment on what the organization is primarily about.

Mission statements should be no longer than ONE SENTENCE. They should be specific and to-the-point. Mission statements that go on and on are a turn-off for most employees. Who wants to learn a declaration two paragraphs long? Keep your mission statement elementary.

> **Our mission at Hamburger Haven is to provide fast, quality food at an affordable price.**

Simple, but effective. Employees have a guideline for performance. They know that their job is not only to prepare a fast hamburger, but a quality hamburger made with pride.

Mission statements do not need to be boring. I once read a mission statement for a training and education department that went like this:

> **Our mission in education and training is to boldly take training and development where no one has taken it before.**

How about this one:

> **Our mission at Lambert Hotels is to make our hotel a home-away-from-home where our customer's needs are not just met, but exceeded.**

Here's a hotel that doesn't want to just satisfy its customers, but delight them. Each employee knows it is his or her job to exceed customer expectations. It's a standard to be met.

Vision Statement

Every organization should also have a vision statement. This statement brings employees into alignment on where the company desires to be in the future. A vision statement should also be delivered in one sentence.

> **Our vision at Hamburger Haven is to be the fast food place of choice in the local community.**

Most vision statements have something to do with being #1 — #1 in the community, the state, the nation, or internationally.

Mission and vision statements are part of the standards used to govern performance and behavior. But more is needed, as it's difficult to measure performance and behavior against a mission or vision statement alone.

Job Descriptions

Every employee in any organization, with the possible exception of the highest levels of management, must have a job description that outlines exactly what performance is expected. Job descriptions give managers something to measure performance against. It is never enough to say to an employee, "You're doing a lousy job." What does 'lousy job' mean? This kind of ungrounded statement can ruin a manager's credibility.

Here are job descriptions for employees at Hamburger Haven:

Employee will make hamburgers.

Employee will take orders from customers.

Employee will ensure a safe environment.

Employee will report to work on time as schedule dictates.

As you can see, job descriptions tend to be somewhat generic in nature, simply letting the employee know what tasks he or she is being hired to do. Which brings us to performance standards.

Performance Standards

Performance standards give clear direction on how to accomplish the many aspects of the job description:

Job Description:	Employee will prepare hamburgers.
Performance Standard:	Employee will cook meat at 160 degrees for 5 minutes in convection oven.
Performance Standard:	Employee will use produce that is less than 48 hours old. Produce more than 48 hours old will be discarded immediately.

Do you see how specific performance standards must be? They are measurable and objective. They give employees clear direction on what performance is expected. They also give managers clear standards by which to assess an employee's performance. Technical manuals fall under this category. Customer service jobs that require employees to talk on the phone all day should have measurable terminology, such as:

Employee will make a minimum of 5 sales a day.

Customer wait on phone will not exceed 3 minutes.

Customer drop-off rate will not exceed 5 percent.

Policy and Procedure Handbook

Every organization must have a policy and procedure handbook, outlining standards on drug and alcohol abuse, dress code, safety policies, and the like. If your company has zero tolerance toward drug abuse, then you must uphold that policy. If there is a dress code, you must uphold that policy. One of the main jobs of a manager is to maintain organizational standards.

A company that refurbishes batteries had a lackluster safety section in their policy and procedure handbook. They had no requirements for the wearing of safety hats in dangerous work areas. One day a battery fell on the head of a young man and crushed his skull. He had a wife and two children. His widow sued the company and won. She received a multi-million dollar settlement. That company lost because it didn't have a standard to protect its own employees.

Measure Employee Behavior Through Core Values

Should certain behavior be required from employees toward their internal and external customers? Absolutely! This brings us to one of the most important measurement tools needed in every organization: core values.

Core values set the standards of behavior for an organization. They describe what behaviors are expected and what behaviors are not tolerated. If we're to create environments of excellence to work in, certain behaviors must be expected from each employee. Such as these core values of Hamburger Haven:

We will help each other; we will go out of our way to provide extra support to fellow employees.

We will work jointly to resolve disagreements in a constructive manner.

We will avoid negative behaviors and comments.

We will contribute constructively and positively by exercising the highest level of professional and ethical behavior.

Each team member is empowered and trusted to handle customer needs and problems to the best of his or her ability.

We will treat all customers with respect and exceed the customers' expectations.

By creating, implementing, and upholding its core values, Hamburger Haven has given its employees clear direction on what behaviors are expected. Anything less will not be tolerated.

Do you have behavioral problems in your organization? Is negativity or disrespect allowed? If so, you may be lacking core values. Either that, or your core values are not being taken seriously.

Marriott Hotels takes its core values seriously. New employees are oriented on the core values and are expected to know them. Poor behavior is measured against the core values and is not tolerated. Marriott has learned, like so many other great organizations, that giving clear standards on expected behaviors, and upholding those standards, is one of the best ways to delight its internal and external customers.

Get Employees on the Right Track from the Very Beginning

During the initial interview with a prospective employee, the interviewer should provide the applicant with hard copies of the mission and vision statements, and the core values of the organization. To ensure that the applicant is aware of what behaviors are expected, and that he or she must become aligned to the purpose and vision of the company, these standards should be thoroughly discussed during the first interview.

During orientation, the manager should give the new employee copies of the mission and vision statements, job descriptions, performance standards, policy and procedure handbook, and core values. Once the employee confirms his or her understanding of these standards, the copies are signed by both the employee and manager, and then placed in the employee's personnel file.

Look at what you now have at your disposal! Documents testifying that the employee knows the job and the behaviors expected of him. You can now measure performance and behavior against signed standards.

Without clear direction, employees will lose their allegiance and loyalty.

Measurable standards give our employees the clear and specific direction they need to do their jobs well. Without measurable standards, employees are apt to be confused and frustrated.

Poor Management IS the Root Cause of Most Employee Difficulties

Do you remember this statistic from the introduction of the book? 80% of problems in organizations today are due to management inadequacies. This tells us poor management is the main cause of employee difficulties. Management research through the years has proven that most employees want to do a good job. In the proper environment, they will be motivated and inspired to do the jobs they were hired to do, and do them well.

A lack of measurable standards is one of the main culprits of low productivity and unacceptable employee behavior. Other root causes of poor performance and behavior are:

- **Lack of Resources.** By not providing our employees with the supplies, equipment, time, money, or staffing to do their jobs, we will frustrate our employees and cause roadblocks in their attempts to get the job done.

- **Lack of Training.** Failure to orient the employee to the dynamics and culture of the organization or to adequately train the employee to do the job sets up your employee for possible failure down the road.

Use this three-step program of excellence when training:

Step 1: Show the employee how to perform the task.

Step 2: Have the employee show you how to do it.

Step 3: Have the employee train you how to do the task.

Step three is often overlooked. We train an employee, they show us how to do it, and then we think they're ready to go. But when an employee can teach you how to do the task, that's when he really knows how to do it.

- **Lack of a Healthy Work Environment.** If you have lack of effective communication, a lack of praise and recognition, or a lack of management awareness about how employees feel toward their jobs and the company, don't expect great perform-ance or behavior from your employees. In a home environment it's the parents'—not the child's—responsibility to set the tone. In the work environment it's the manager's—not the employee's—responsibility to set the tone.

- **Poor Performance Is Tolerated.** Here is one of the most important assertions in this book:

Do not tolerate poor performance or behavior from any employee.

One of the root causes of poor performance and behavior in many organizations is that management tolerates employees who behave badly or do not do their jobs. Worse yet, there's no consistency on how such matters are handled. One manager might allow an employee to frequently arrive late, while another manager within the same organization terminates an employee for showing up late only twice.

This is why measurable standards are so important. Meeting expec-tations should be part of an organization's cultural norm.

Be Firm and Cut Your Losses

Organizations are only as successful as the employees who work there.

Managers need to groom and mentor their best employees, while not tolerating poor performance or behavior from substandard employees. Here are some tips for dealing with poor performers:

- **Do Not Keep Employees Who Continue to Spread Negativity.** Do not keep an employee who may have great skills and experience but a lousy attitude. If you've created a great environment to work in, you'll have employees busting the door down to come work for you. Don't waste time, energy, or money attempting to facilitate change in employees who simply do not want to change.

- **Cut Your Losses.** If your sincere coaching and mentoring efforts fail, take that employee aside and let him know he'll be looking for another job soon if he doesn't meet standards. Ask yourself, "Are the costs outweighing the benefits of keeping this person?" and "Is this person worth keeping?" If your answer is no, it may be time to proceed toward terminating the relationship. Don't be held hostage by employees who have good technical skills but horrible behaviors that destroy morale. CUT YOUR LOSSES! It's all part of being an effective manager.

This can be easy to say and tough to do. You may have an employee who is a real pain but outperforms the rest. This person might be very hard to replace due to his or her technical expertise, or the lack of a solid employee pool in your community. No matter how hard cutting your losses may be, you must remember this old adage:

The bed you make, you must sleep in.

If management decides to keep a stellar performer who is destroying morale through poor behavior, then management must accept the fact that there will be major morale and performance issues with other employees. There's no getting around it. When performance plummets, management is ultimately to blame. But let me give you some hope in this situation. Hundreds of managers have tried this tactic and it almost always works.

A manager at a training workshop shared her story. "Hal, I agree with you one hundred percent about cutting losses. I had to do it a few months ago. One employee was my best performer and had the highest technical skills, but her behavior was horrible. Employees were ready to quit. I made coaching efforts with this employee, and gave her verbal and written warnings, but she still refused to change. I knew I needed to terminate her, but I was afraid to because she would be very hard to replace. Her knowledge of the job was incredible. I let things go for a while and it continued to get worse. Finally, I let her go. I didn't sleep all night because I was so worried about replacing her. I'd even looked for a replacement before terminating her, but I couldn't find one.

"When I went to work the next day, my other employees were waiting for me at the door. When they saw me, they clapped and cheered. One said, 'It's about time she got canned. She was horrible to work with.' Another employee said, 'Now we can finally have the high morale we've always wanted around this place. Now we can be a team.'

"My employees shook my hand and told me how gutsy I was. They all said they would be willing to work later, come in earlier, and do whatever it would take to cover that position until I could find a replacement. It was like a huge weight had been lifted from the department, and I found a replacement a few months later. Meanwhile, my employees worked as a team to handle the extra workload because they were finally rid of the bad apple."

Be the Glue You Were Hired to Be

You are the glue in your department. It's your job to make sure your employees are doing the jobs they were hired to do. Committing yourself to the strategies in this book will guarantee your success.

Most of the time, poor performance or behavior are due to a lack of effective management. Sometimes it is due to an employee's poor work ethic. Yes, there are slackers out there who want to do the bare minimum and still get a paycheck, but these employees are not the norm. Sometimes poor performance is partly due to management and partly due to the employee. No matter what the root cause of the poor performance or behavior, it cannot be allowed to continue. It must be dealt with in a timely manner.

Do you have any employees who are not doing their jobs well? Do you have an employee whose negative attitude is spreading like a cancer?

Don't despair! Help is just the flip of a page away. In this chapter we discussed the importance of having measurable standards and how management contributes to poor performance and behavior. In the next chapter, you will learn the #1 way to deal with unacceptable employee performance and behavior.

Action Plan – Reality Check

Is Management Doing Its Job in Your Organization?

1. My organization has a one-sentence mission statement .... ❏ Yes ❏ No

2. Employees are expected to know the mission statement .... ❏ Yes ❏ No

3. My organization has a one-sentence vision statement ❏ Yes ❏ No

4. Employees are expected to know the vision statement ❏ Yes ❏ No

5. Employees have clear, specific job descriptions ..... ❏ Yes ❏ No

6. Employees have clear, specific performance standards ❏ Yes ❏ No

7. My organization has a policy and procedure handbook .... ❏ Yes ❏ No

8. Employees are required to know policies that relate to them .... ❏ Yes ❏ No

9. My organization has clear, specific core values ..... ❏ Yes ❏ No

10. Employees are required to know core values ...... ❏ Yes ❏ No

11. Mission, Vision and Core Values are discussed during interview .... ❏ Yes ❏ No

Employees have signed copies of these in their personnel folders:

1. Mission statement .... ❏ Yes ❏ No

2. Vision statement .... ❏ Yes ❏ No

3. Core values .... ❏ Yes ❏ No

4. Job descriptions .... ❑ Yes ❑ No

5. Performance standards .... ❑ Yes ❑ No

6. Policy and procedure handbook .... ❑ Yes ❑ No

7. My organization provides employees with adequate
   resources .... ❑ Yes ❑ No

8. My organization provides adequate orientation
   and training .... ❑ Yes ❑ No

9. My organization provides a healthy work
   environment .... ❑ Yes ❑ No

10. Poor performance is not tolerated and is dealt with
    in a timely manner .... ❑ Yes ❑ No

Tally the Yes answers _____

Tally the No answers _____

What can you do as a proactive leader in your organization to turn each No into a Yes?

Make copies of this test and then ask personnel in your human resources department to take the test. If you feel comfortable, ask some in top management to take it. It may be an eye opener and bring about the changes needed to make your company even better.

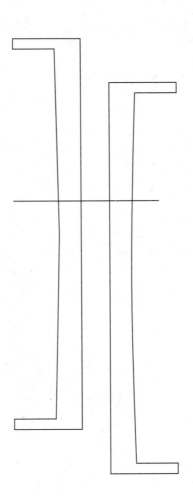

CHAPTER 17

The #1 Way to Deal with Poor Performance or Behavior

Every manager encounters employees who do not do the jobs they were hired to do. In Chapter 16 you discovered that poor management is the root cause of most employee difficulties. Lack of training. Lack of resources. Inadequate standards. Lack of empowerment and ownership. A boss who doesn't Manage by Wandering Around. These all add up to poor productivity and behavior.

No matter what the reason for poor performance or behavior, it must be dealt with. Problems swept under the rug will escalate into bigger problems.

There is only ONE WAY to effectively deal with poor performance and behavior. There is only ONE WAY to give your employees an opportunity to excel and redirect their behavior.

What is the #1 way to deal with poor performance or behavior?

TURN THE PAGE TO FIND OUT! ☞

The Number One Secrets of Successful Managers

The #1 Way to Deal with
Poor Performance or Behavior Is...

Talk
About It

Talking About the Problem IS the Answer

Were you waiting for some earth-shattering strategy? You don't need one. The best way to get to the root of an employee's poor performance or behavior is to have a one-on-one meeting to get to the bottom of things. There's no way around it.

Talk Is the Answer

Speaking with an employee about his or her substandard performance or behavior can be a scary proposition. But it's the only way to resolve employee problems. A manager who allows substandard performance or behavior to continue is not managing effectively.

Don't go home angry or frustrated about an employee's poor performance or behavior. Deal with the issue right away to avoid even greater problems in the future.

Important Tips to Know
BEFORE You Meet With an Employee

These tips will give you confidence and help you communicate your thoughts more effectively.

Remember: You Are the Boss

You were given positional power by your organization for just such an occasion. You do not need to be intimidated by any employee at any time. Relax. You have the power.

Talk with the employee privately

Never discuss employee issues in front of others. It is not fair to that employee and can potentially hurt your credibility. If you show others respect, they will return that respect. As the old saying goes, "Praise in public, criticize in private."

See yourself as giving the person an Opportunity to Grow

When you talk with employees about their poor performance or behavior, do not view the meeting as a time of criticism. View the meeting as a time to give them every opportunity to grow and excel in the organization. You're not behind closed doors to badger or to undermine self-esteem. You're there to give your employee positive feedback about how he or she can improve and be more successful.

View your management position as that of a coach and a facilitator. See yourself as having the tools to help your employees succeed. This new perception of yourself will turn these once-scary meetings into opportunities to facilitate positive change in others.

Get to the purpose quickly

Don't be apologetic. Don't hem and haw. Get quickly to the purpose of the meeting, deal with the issue, and get the employee back to work. Time is money.

Always direct feedback toward the action, not the person

Respect the rights of others. Don't blast employees with their perceived shortcomings. Don't use subjective statements such as, "You're doing a lousy job" or "You never do anything right around here." These statements attack the person's character and your emotional bank account will quickly go bankrupt. Remember that you don't have the means to change anyone. You can only offer salt tablets to make them thirsty for the refreshing waters of good performance and behavior.

Deal with the Problem in a Timely Manner

If you observe a person not doing his or her job, don't let the day end without discussing it. Do not wait! Tackle it while the situation or issue is still fresh in both of your minds.

Meetings that Get Results

What follows is a step-by-step approach to effective communication—one that you can use in just about every meeting you have with your employees concerning poor performance or behavior.

To help illustrate this approach, let's assume that you're a manager at Hamburger Haven, with fifteen employees working the day shift.

One of your employees is Joey, age twenty-seven, who has worked at Hamburger Haven for three months. He is showing a new employee named Sue how to make a hamburger. You walk around the corner and observe the following:

Joey doesn't cook the meat long enough. It's blood rare.

Joey places some wilted lettuce on the hamburger.

Joey flips the meat in the air to show off. A portion of the meat breaks off. He puts it on the bun anyway.

Joey puts the meal on the tray and calls the customer's number.

Is there a problem with Joey's performance and behavior? If so, how do you know? What do you measure his actions against? When would you talk with Joey?

First, you must make sure that the hamburger does not get to the customer in its current condition. Next, Joey should be in your office... NOW! Not at the end of the shift, not the next day, but now, while the problem is fresh. Joey is not doing the job he was hired to do, and he could have caused the loss of a customer.

Now is the time to have a meeting with Joey. There should be two parts to your meeting: stating the problem, and the action plan.

Stating the Problem

First, state the problem simply.

Let Joey know why he is in the office.

"Joey, the reason I've called you into my office is because of what I observed just now while you were making a hamburger."

Next, state the problem with specifics.

"Joey, this is what I observed. I saw you put a rare hamburger on the bun. I saw you put wilted lettuce on the hamburger. I saw you flip the meat in the air like pizza dough. I saw meat break off and you put it back anyway."

State the standards that were violated, and the impact that the performance or behavior has on others and the organization.

"Joey, as you know, by not cooking the meat to our temperature standards, you could possibly make the customer sick. By putting wilted lettuce on the bun, we could have lost that customer by providing an inferior product. Our performance standards state that any produce more than 48 hours old should be discarded. When you flipped the meat in the air, the customer could have spotted your behavior and walked out. As you know, one of our core values states that employees will take pride in their work and act like owners. One more thing, Joey. You were orienting Sue to her new job. I'm sure you'd agree that your behavior wasn't setting a good example."

State the performance or behavior you desire to see in the future.

"Joey, these are company expectations for every employee. Cook all meat according to standards, take pride in your work and act like an owner, and follow performance standards concerning the use of produce."

Get employee input.

One reason some managers do not get the desired results is due to a lack of participation by the employee. As covered in Chapter 9, the #1 way to gain employee commitment is through involvement. Get your employee involved by allowing him to clarify his position. Don't do all the talking. Allow your employee to express his opinion.

Now that you've stated the problem and clarified your own position, it's time to hear what Joey has to say. Here are a few phrases you can use to encourage employee input:

"What do you think about what I said?"

"Do you understand why there's a problem with your performance?"

"What do you think about my position on this matter?"

"How do you see the problem?"

During meetings with your employees, be willing to see their side of the story. Seek to understand where they're coming from. Ask questions and solicit their feedback.

Let's say that after discussing the matter, Joey owns up to his poor performance and behavior (which will not always be the case) and says, "You're right boss. I shouldn't have flipped the meat in the air. I should have cooked the meat like we're supposed to, and I should have trashed the old lettuce and put new lettuce on the bun. I apologize."

You've now completed the first part of the process. You have stated your position specifically and how the poor performance will impact the organization. You also clarified the performance desired in the future and solicited employee feedback.

Now it's time for the second part of the process.

The Action Plan

Discuss Solutions.

Whenever possible, have the employee come up with the solution. By doing so, you're holding the person accountable for his or her performance, and thus, facilitating ownership and leadership.

"I'm glad you realize you weren't following standards. What is a good action plan we can write down so this doesn't happen again?"

Here are more phrases you can use to show your employee that you're interested in solving the problem together:

> **"Here's how I think we should proceed. What do you think?"**
>
> **"Let's take a look at the solutions together."**
>
> **"What do you suggest can be done to keep this from happening again?"**
>
> **"Is this a solution you can commit to in writing?"**

Write Down Solutions.

Now begins the documentation phase of the meeting. Write down the actions that Joey — and you as his manager, if need be — will take to ensure standards are met. Your human resource department probably has a standard form for coaching or performance improvement sessions.

One of the main reasons performance improvement meetings may fail is due to lack of a written action plan. Perhaps you've heard the old management saying, "If it wasn't written, it wasn't done."

Both Sign Documentation

Once the action plan is in writing, both you and your employee should sign the document. In many cases, there may be need for a follow-up. Document when the follow-up will take place, and document the follow-up itself. The documentation goes into the employee's personnel file.

If the employee refuses to sign, you may want to get your boss or someone from HR to witness you noting on the document that the employee refused to sign. Many companies simply have the manager write down a statement that the employee refused to sign, and have the employee initial the statement. In today's society, where some employees may sue a company for the pettiest of reasons, documentation is a must.

When Coaching Doesn't Work

What do you do when an employee continues to break the rules? You have coached and mentored, but the employee refuses to change and you're not getting the return on the investment you've made in this employee.

If the cost of poor performance or behavior continues to outweigh the benefit, it's time to discipline the employee. This book cannot address the proper disciplinary procedure for all organizations, such as union settings, civil service, state and federal agencies. Visit your human resources department to ensure you are following proper procedures for disciplining employees. Below are the procedures that many companies follow. Let us use Joey again as an example to show how this works.

The first time you had a meeting with Joey concerning his poor hamburger making, you coached him and together you developed a written action plan for performance improvement. He signed the coaching effort and it was placed in his personnel file.

Two weeks later, you observe Joey again flipping a hamburger in the air. Now it's time for a verbal warning.

Verbal Warning

Have another meeting with Joey. Follow the same procedure that you did with the first meeting:

"Joey, the reason I've called you into my office today is because I again observed you flipping a hamburger in the air inappropriately. Today I am giving you a verbal warning."

Talk to Joey about the standards not followed, the consequences of the behavior, and the behavior you desire in the future. Get Joey's input. Once again, devise a plan of action, write it down, and have both of you sign it.

Smart managers form strong partnerships with their bosses and their human resource departments. Ensure that HR and your boss are aware of the verbal warning.

If again, two weeks after the verbal warning, you observe Joey not cooking the meat according to specifications, it's time for a written warning.

Written Warning

Have another meeting with Joey. Let him know he's receiving a written warning for his actions. Follow the same meeting steps as with the verbal warning. Discuss an action plan, document it, and place it in Joey's file.

Most businesses use the "Three strikes and you're out" rule. If one or two coaching efforts fail, most organizations give employees first a verbal warning, then a written warning, and then proceed to termination.

One week after the written warning, Joey is working at the counter. He gets upset with a customer and starts calling the customer names. It's time for termination.

Termination

This is your last meeting with Joey. Call him into the office with a witness present. The witness can be someone from HR, your boss, or a manager from another department. Go through the meeting process again, except this time the action plan is termination. Do not back down and do not be apologetic. Remember this:

Managers DO NOT terminate employees.
Employees terminate themselves.

Have Joey's paycheck ready and escort him, with the witness, to his car and watch him leave. Never allow an employee to wander the building after termination. You never know what the employee will say or do.

You are now rid of an employee who was doing your organization more harm than good. Termination is not fun, but it is necessary when an employee refuses to meet organizational expectations.

The "What Ifs" in Talking with Employees

The above meeting examples with Joey are not realistic as to how your meetings might proceed. Most meetings rarely go that smoothly. Here are a few "What Ifs" to help you field the curve balls:

What If an employee starts blaming everyone else?

This is one of the most common reactions. Employees begin blaming fellow employees, using defenses such as: "Well, so and so is doing the same thing" or "No one else seems to get in trouble but me."

When an employee starts down the blaming path, immediately bring his behavior back into focus. Do not let the person get you sidetracked. Tell the employee this meeting is for positive feedback—that you're aware of other situations and are taking care of business. Remind blaming employees that they are accountable for their own poor performance or behavior, regardless of what others may be doing.

What if an employee refuses the action plan?

Make sure you've remained open to the possibility of your own mismanagement or other mitigating circumstances. But if an employee is stubborn and refuses to develop an action plan during the meeting, stand your ground and come up with the solution yourself.

The time will come during a meeting with an employee when you may have to say something like this:

"Stan, I've done everything I can during our meeting to help you devise an action plan to meet standards. I have talked with you informally on many occasions to give you guidance, but you refuse to listen. So here's my plan of action. Either you allow me to help you with your performance issue, or the next time it happens you'll be given a verbal warning. If you continue performing this way, you may find yourself without a job. Is there anything you'd like to say before I write this on the action plan?"

Here's another tactic you can use with an employee who refuses to respond to the opportunities you offer:

"Jane, the reason I've called you into my office today is because of the way you treated Nancy. I overheard you calling her a worthless idiot. Jane, I have had to talk with you on several other occasions, a few of them with documentation, about your crass attitude toward coworkers. And it's going to stop today. So, I'd like you to grab your things and go on home for the rest of the day. I'll cover your position for the last couple of hours. You're to meet me in my office tomorrow at eight a.m. with your answer. Starting tomorrow, you'll come to work with a professional attitude and be a team player, or seek employment elsewhere."

What if my employee is the best worker but has a bad attitude?

Behavioral problems must be dealt with exactly like performance problems. Coach and mentor the employee who is abrasive toward coworkers or acts unprofessionally. Use your company's core values as the standards to measure behavior.

If the poor behavior persists after a couple of coaching efforts, give the employee a verbal warning, a written warning, and then proceed to termination. Do not waste time on those who undermine morale. Weed them out quickly.

What if I have a boss who keeps giving my department more work than we can handle?

Use the "pass the monkey" strategy. Make your boss responsible for your success. That's what your boss is there for: to partner with you in developing strategies that get the best performance from employees. If your boss gives you too many unrealistic projects, you have every right to stand your ground and pass the monkey back to your boss by saying no in a tactful way. Here's one way to say NO professionally:

"Boss, I can see how important this new project is. You're also aware that we have four other projects due at the same time. With our current manning shortage, we won't get this project done on deadline. I know you want our department to put out a quality product. So, boss, what can we do here? What project would you like us to table for a while so we can get this new one done on time?"

What if no one in the organization will back me up on a decision I feel strongly about?

It all depends on how badly you want to keep your job. Politics and bureaucracy are alive and well in corporate America. No one can tell you how far to go with your convictions. But I can relate to you a Cinderella story shared by a young woman during a training workshop.

The manager felt strongly about giving an employee a verbal warning. The employee was behaving poorly and putting out an inferior product. She discussed the matter with her boss and he said no to the verbal warning. She continued to document the employee's poor performance and behavior. A week later, she sat down and talked with her boss about the problem employee. He again said no to any disciplinary action.

The employee's performance and behavior became intolerable. The manager set up a meeting with her boss's boss and invited her boss so the three of them could discuss the difficult employee. The boss's boss said no to the verbal warning.

The situation worsened and morale in her department plummeted. She went to the general manager to voice her concerns. The general manager said to let it go and just tolerate the poor performance. The manager documented everything, including her discussions with management.

Finally, she could take no more. The manager loved her company and felt the employee was a detriment to the organization. With her own money, she flew to corporate headquarters and set up a meeting with the CEO. She met with him, showed him the mounds of documentation, and discussed the problems the employee was causing. The CEO was so impressed that she would buy her own plane ticket to talk with him, he said, "You know, you're exactly the kind of person I'm looking for in my company. Someone who is persistent and proactive in making things happen."

She flew back home with no concrete answers. However, things changed quickly. Within a few weeks, the employee and the manager's own boss were terminated. One day later her boss's boss was terminated. The general manager was transferred within a week. And a few days after that, she was promoted to her boss' position with a substantial raise.

Good things can happen to those who are proactive, persistent, and are willing to make waves in a tactful, professional way. Unfortunately, things don't always work out idealistically. Go as far as you feel you can. If you're not in the position to lose your job by making waves, then do not make waves. Attempt other leadership strategies to try to effect changes over time. Be proud of the little things you accomplish in your department. Be proud of that one employee you helped mentor into a true leader. It's all a matter of perspective.

A Most Important Management Lesson

Before ending this chapter, there's one important lesson all managers and employees must learn:

No one forces any employee to work where they work.

If an employee cannot go to work with some level of enthusiasm, it's time for that employee to quit. Whining, negativity, complaining and unprofessional behavior should not be tolerated in any organization. People are hired to do jobs and must be expected to do those jobs well. That's what they're being paid for. It's up to management to create an environment conducive to outstanding performance and behavior.

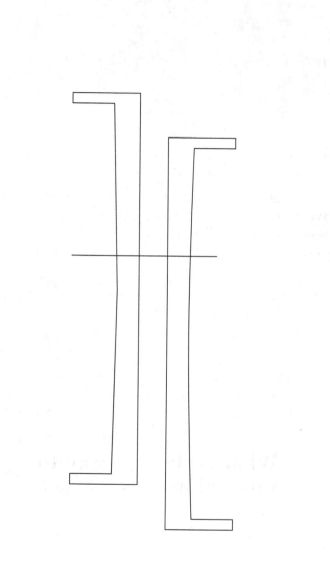

CHAPTER 18

The #1 Way to Succeed as a Manager

In the early nineteenth century, Andrew Carnegie, steel magnate and philanthropist, was asked this question by a newspaperman: "Mr. Carnegie, why are you successful?"

Carnegie thought about this for a moment, and then said, "Sir, I won't give you my answer just yet. I'd first like you to interview other successful people and discover what they have to say. Once you've accomplished this task, ask me again and I'll give you my answer."

The newspaperman took up Carnegie's challenge. Months later, he confronted Carnegie with his results. "Mr. Carnegie, I have done as you asked. I interviewed other successful people to ask them why they are successful."

Carnegie asked for the results and smiled when the journalist gave it. It was the same response he would have given. And that response is the #1 way not only to succeed as a manager, but in life.

What is the #1 way to succeed as a manager?

TURN THE PAGE TO FIND OUT! ☞

The Number One Secrets of Successful Managers

The #1 Way to Succeed
as a Manager Is to...

Surround Yourself with Successful People

Surround Yourself with Successful People

When Andrew Carnegie died, this epitaph was engraved on his tombstone:

*Here lies a man who knew how to enlist
the service of better men than himself.*

Here are some valuable tips on succeeding with and through others.

Find a Mentor

No person is an island.

One of the most important lessons you will ever learn in management is: YOU CANNOT SUCCEED IN MANAGEMENT ON YOUR OWN! It's too difficult. You will confront people and issues that will leave you groping for answers.

Find someone—your boss, a previous boss, a friend or family member—who has management experience and can help you through the rough times. And there WILL be rough times. Lots of them. Gaining peak performance from people is one of the biggest challenges anyone can face. Just ask any parent who tries to get her child to clean his room!

There's nothing more comforting than a few trustworthy mentors you can laugh and cry with, or pound your fist on the wall and scream, "I don't understand what's going on here!"

Another reason for having a mentor is for personal guidance. Don't try to figure out life on your own. Just as talking about it with employees is a #1 method for dealing with problems, so you need mentors of your own to do this with.

Surround Yourself with Positive People

Here's more great management advice: GET AWAY FROM NEGA-TIVE PEOPLE. Stay away from the proverbial water cooler where people gather to do nothing but moan and complain about every-one and everything.

Negative people tear down an organization. Their whining can spread like a cancer, infecting departments and destroying morale.

Surround yourself with people who desire to do something with their lives. Surround yourself with people who have vision and pas-sion for living.

Martin Luther King, Jr. once said,

"If a man hasn't discovered something he will die for, he isn't fit to live."

Help negative people see the light of optimism through your own example of excellence. Make them responsible for developing solu-tions to problems, instead of being part of the problem.

The Power of Interpersonal Linkages

Wouldn't it be wonderful if all your hard work and expertise guar-anteed success in life? Unfortunately, such is rarely the case. Sweat, toil and persistence are necessary to reach one's true potential and dreams, but hard work does not always translate into attainment. There's another element needed to ensure you succeed, not only in management but in life.

It's not what you know, but who you know.

The word "networking" has been around for quite some time. Take any career-planning course and the word is mentioned repeatedly.

Networking is the art of schmoozing. Networking is talking with anyone about anything. Networking allows you to build interpersonal linkages with a multitude of people who may be able to help you at any given time in your life. It also affords you the opportunity to help others in their time of need.

Building interpersonal linkages with others in your organization is an absolute must to succeed in management. By doing so, you will build a strong power base for yourself by virtue of who you know. Building relationships with others in your organization will help you get things done with and through people who have the resources to get you what you need.

To build this absolutely essential power base, you must get out of your office and get to know people. If you have the chance to build a relationship with your CEO, by all means, do so. If you have a chance to go to meetings and develop rapport with people in high places, take advantage of the opportunity.

Go to company picnics. Attend functions where you can schmooze with other managers and develop partnerships. Help everyone you can. Management is all about people helping people, and building those all-important relationships.

I hear hundreds of success stories every year about the importance of networking and building interpersonal linkages. Here are just a few:

> " I had a chance to get to know our general manager. We formed a strong professional relationship. Over time, I found people started treating me differently. Some started asking if I could talk to the GM about this or that. In meetings, people asked for my opinion more. I found I was able to get resources I was never able to get before. And all because of my knowing the head honcho."

> " I was downsized in my organization. Job prospects in my community were bleak and I was to the point of despair when I started talking with a man as we stood in line to see a movie. The next thing, he was offering me a job at his company making more than I did at my previous job."

" I was out of work for two months. I've never been a talker, but decided I needed to start talking with people because you never know whom you're talking to. I was sitting next to a woman on the bus and we hit it off. She worked for a company in their human resources department. She invited me in for an interview and I got a job within the week."

Much of our success in life will be dependent on who we know, not what we know. Take a look at Hollywood. There are thousands of starving waiters and waitresses who have just as much talent as the mega-movie stars, but may never get a break because they don't know the right people.

Talk with People You Don't Know

Are you timid when it comes to talking with others? If so, it's time to step outside of your comfort zone and start conversing with people. Send people you know a birthday or thank you card once in a while. Don't expect people to come to you. Get out there and show your face. Like Mae West said, "Honey, it's better to be looked over than overlooked."

Here's another great saying when it comes to networking:

*A person who would have friends must
show himself or herself to be friendly.*

The most effective managers are accessible and friendly. They do not stay stuck in their offices, but get out into their organizations and build interpersonal linkages. They know where to go and whom to talk to in order to get employees the resources they need to do their jobs. By doing so, they help ensure the success of their employees.

Action Plan

Who Is Helping You Become Successful?

Write down the name(s) of your mentor(s):

1. _____

2. _____

3. _____

If you don't have one, find a mentor within one month.

Today's date _____ Date you'll have a mentor _____

Write down the names of five people, besides family, who are having a positive impact on your life right now, and are available to help you set goals and strategies in your life.

1. _____

2. _____

3. _____

4. _____

5. _____

If you can't think of five people, it's time to start developing interpersonal linkages with more people.

Write down the names of five managers with whom you have formed interpersonal linkages.

1. _____

2. _____

3. _____

4. _____

5. _____

If you can't think of five, it's time to get out of your office and start networking.

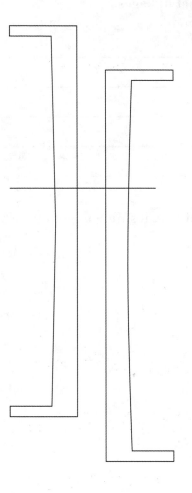

CHAPTER 19

The #1 Reason for Wanting to Be a Manager

Why would anyone in his or her right mind want to be a manager? The pay is not always commensurate with the responsibilities, difficulties arise almost every day, and there will always be a certain level of ineptitude with various people in upper management.

I have often asked myself why I enjoy being a manager. One reason is the challenge of getting results when people say it cannot be done. Another is the satisfaction of using the various leadership and management strategies talked about in this book to get performance from someone who is labeled "difficult" or "a troublemaker." Another reason I enjoy being a manager is working with great men and women, who are proactive and persistent in making good things happen.

But of all the reasons I can think of for wanting to be a manager, one is always foremost in my mind. This reason has nothing to do with money or making the boss happy. It has nothing to do with performance or getting results. It does not even have to do with necessarily liking my job. Everyone hates his job once in a while.

The #1 reason I want to be a manager is based more in philosophical spheres than business. It's what drives me more than anything else to get out there every morning and deal with employees on a day-to-day basis. And I've met many other managers who share this view.

If you find you are frustrated being a manager due to bureaucracy or perceived unfairness, maybe this #1 reason for wanting to be a manager will help you reframe how you perceive your position and give you a positive slant on the daily grind of management. So, what is the #1 reason for wanting to be a manager?

TURN THE PAGE TO FIND OUT! ☞

The Number One Secrets of Successful Managers

The #1 Reason for
Wanting to Be a Manager Is...

You Can
Make a
Difference!

*"Besides raising a family,
there is no place on earth a person can have
more of a positive impact on the lives of others
than as a manager at work."*

—HAL PITT

Think about it. Besides the time you spend with your family and friends, where do you spend most of your time? At work, of course. I know managers who spend more time at work than with their loved ones. And because of the amount of time you spend working with and managing others, think of the powerful impact you have on your internal and external customers every day.

As a manager, you impact the lives of those you work with on a daily basis. Every word you speak, every deed you perform has a consequence. It's your choice whether your words and actions will be helpful or hurtful; will build-up or tear down.

You have incredible power as a manager. You have the power to reward and the power to punish. You have the power to make good things happen and the power to crush the morale in your department. The best managers use their power toward an earnest pursuit of getting results through people, while at the same time commanding the respect of others.

Reflect on yourself as a manager right now. Are you commanding the respect of others through your actions and words? Do people come to you for advice because you can be trusted? Is your good name known throughout the organization?

Commit yourself to making a positive impact on those you manage and on others in your organization. Doing the right thing can be its own reward. The joy you can derive from management lies in your point of view. If you view management as the laborious task of getting results from people who don't want to work hard, you will hate management and ultimately fail at it. But, if you view management as a wonderful opportunity to get results through people while impacting their lives in a positive way, you will find management fulfilling and will ultimately succeed. Management has a way of testing our mettle — it helps us discover what we're truly made of.

As a management trainer and consultant, I've had the opportunity to hear hundreds of stories throughout the country from managers who have had powerful impacts on their employees. Yet of all the stories I've heard, none is as powerful as the one I was told in Tulsa, Oklahoma.

During a management seminar I made this closing statement about making a difference in our employees' lives. "The chances of walking in to work tomorrow and receiving accolades from your employees about the positive impact you've had on their lives is pretty slim. Just take heart that you're doing everything in your power to do it right."

After making that statement, two women in the front row raised their hands to get my attention. One of the women said, "Hal, do you mind if we disagree with you?"

Now, I don't mind being disagreed with, but these women looked like they had something fervent to say. I got ready for a verbal assault. "Of course not," I said. "What do you disagree with?"

The women who had addressed me stood up. "Hal, do you mind if I share something?"

Now I was getting a little nervous. She seemed intent on saying something to the group. I looked into her eyes to try and get a sense of her demeanor. I saw tears well up in her eyes. "By all means," I said, "Please share with us."

The woman turned to the group and said, "I just want to reaffirm everything Hal has been saying today. That it is possible to be an outstanding manager and make a difference in your employees' lives. You see, my boss just died last week of cancer. He was the greatest boss one could ever ask for. He did everything Hal has been talking about today. He Managed by Wandering Around. He recognized and praised our efforts. He was always there to listen to us and he made us feel important and valued. We would have gone to the ends of the earth for that man if he had asked us to.

"We loved that man so much we got permission from our general manager to close our department for the day. All the employees in the department carpooled down to the hospital and we received permission from the special care nurse to visit him in his room. His family was there and he was in a coma. We all squeezed into that tiny room and gathered around his bed. Then, holding hands together with his family, we took turns telling him how much we loved him, how much we would miss him, and how irreplaceable he was in our lives."

The woman turned and grabbed a tissue from her friend's hand. She wiped her eyes, and then said, "When almost all of us were through saying how much we respected him, he died."

The woman sat down. I leaned on a chair and just stood silent. The audience didn't say a word. I could only think of one more thing to say to close the workshop. "Ladies and gentleman, I stand corrected. Maybe we can do this management stuff so right—maybe we can have such a positive impact on the lives of others—that when we're on our deathbeds, our employees will come to us and say, 'You were the best boss I ever had.'"

Action Plan–Time for Reflection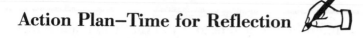

Give yourself credit

Think of a time when someone told you that you made a difference in his or her life. Write down what that person said:

_____

_____

_____

_____

_____

Think of another time when someone told you that you made a difference in his or her life. Write down what that person said:

_____

_____

_____

_____

_____

Think of another time when someone told you that you made a difference in his or her life. Write down what that person said:

_____

_____

_____

_____

_____

As you were writing, what emotions did you feel when remembering what each person said?

_____

_____

_____

_____

_____

Feels good, doesn't it?

Keep up the good work!

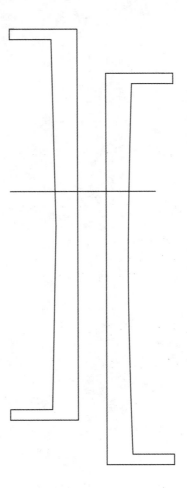

CHAPTER 20

The Number Ones Revisited

By reading this book, you have gained important information about effectively managing others. Hopefully, you've discovered new lessons and revisited old ones. Maybe you have new insights about your strengths and weaknesses as a manager.

Now it's time to revisit what you have learned. Reading this book one time is not enough. To get the full benefit of what you've read, you will need to reread the book a few times and commit yourself to practicing the lessons. You will need to follow through on the exercises at the end of each chapter.

Test your knowledge on what you've learned by completing the exercise below. Do not write in the answers; mentally see how much you can remember. Find the answers in the book if you have forgotten some of the information. Do this over and over until you can quickly and easily answer all the questions.

1. What is the #1 job of every manager?

2. What is the #1 purpose of every organization?

3. We can no longer merely satisfy customers.
   We must _____ them.

4. What is the #1 management concept of all time?

5. What is the #1 goal of every manager?

6. What is the theory of critical mass as applied to management?

7. What is the #1 way to reach your #1 goal?

8. What are the three rights of proper delegation?

9. What is the #1 attitude every manager must have?

10. What is the #1 way to motivate and retain most employees?

11. What is the #1 way to motivate every employee?

12. What is the #1 way to gain employee commitment?

13. What is the #1 reason most employees quit?

14. What is the #1 leadership strategy of all time?

15. List four other leadership strategies.

16. What is the #1 quality every leader must have?

17. What is the #1 way to lead?

18. What is the #1 problem in most organizations?

19. What is the #1 way to reduce stress in the workplace?

20. What is the #1 reason for poor performance and behavior?

21. "If it can't be _____, it can't be _____."

22. What is the #1 way to deal with poor performance and behavior?

23. What is the #1 way to succeed as a manager?

24. What is the #1 reason for wanting to be a manager in the first place?

How did you do? If you're like most adult learners, you were lucky to answer sixty percent of the questions. Keep revisiting until you know them by heart.

Good luck in all your management endeavors. Commit yourself to excellence and keep learning all you can about managing others. It's a tough job but you are up to the task.

The Number One Secrets of Successful Managers

BIBLIOGRAPHY

BOOKS

Bennis, Warren & Burt Nanus. *Leaders: The Strategies for Taking Charge.* New York: Harper & Row, Publishers, 1985.

Caldini, Robert B. *Influence: Science and Practice*, 3rd Edition. Harper Collins College Publishers, 1993.

Covey, Stephen. *The 7 Habits of Highly Effective People.* Simon & Schuster, 1989.

Friedman, Paul. *How to Deal With Difficult People.* SkillPath Publications, 1994.

Grout, Pam. *The Mentoring Advantage.* SkillPath Publications, 1995.

Hackman, Michael Z. & Craig E. Johnson. *Leadership: A Communication Perspective.* Waveland Press, Inc., 1991.

Holpp, Lawrence. *Managing Teams.* McGraw-Hill, 1999.

Knight, Sue. *NLP and Work.* London: Nicholas Brealey Publishing, 1999.

Lieberman, David J. *Make Peace With Anyone.* New York: St. Martin's Press, 2002.

Lewis, Pamela S., Stephen H. Goodman and Patricia M Fandt. *Management: Challenges in the 21st Century*, 2nd Edition. South-Western College Publishing, 1998.

Pollan, Stephen M., and Mark Levine. *Lifescripts.* Wiley Publishing, Inc., 1996.

Runion, Meryl. *Power Phrases.* Power Potentials Publishing, 2002.

Schroeder, Joel and Ruth. *The Power of Positivity*.
SkillPath Publications, 1997.

Useem, Michael. *The Leadership Moment*.
New York: Random House, 1998.

Wellins, Richard S., William C. Byham and Jeanne M. Wilson.
Empowered Teams. San Francisco: Jossey Bass Publishers, 1991.

White, Ken R., and Elwood N Chapman.
Organizational Communication.
Simon & Schuster Custom Publishing, 1996.

AUDIOS

Braunstein, Barbara.
Dealing With Different, Diverse (and Difficult) People.
SkillPath Publications, 2001.

Covey, Stephen. *The 7 Habits of Highly Effective People*.
Provo, Utah: Franklin Covey Co., 1997.

Larsen, Linda. *The 12 Secrets to High Self Esteem*.
SkillPath Publications, 1999.

Speaker's Roundtable. *The Pros Speak About Success*.
SkillPath Publications, 1999.

The Number One Secrets of Successful Managers

Who is Hal Pitt?

Hal Pitt
Mile High Leadership
www.milehighleadership.com
Training, Consulting and Keynotes
pitthal@aol.com

Who is Hal Pitt?
- International Speaker
- Published Author
- No Nonsense, Reality-Based Trainer
- University of Northern Colorado Graduate
- Adjunct Professor, Regis University
- Twenty-two Year United States Air Force Veteran

Hal Pitt has:
- A Master's Degree, Communication
- Taught over 300 seminars in the U.S., Canada, Australia, and the U.K.

Hal is available for training and keynotes. He will:
- Help your organization discover what it's doing right and what needs improving.
- Equip managers and supervisors with the skills they need to retain and motivate employees.
- Show employees how to provide outstanding customer service that is key to profitability.

Training Specialties Include:
- Leadership
- Management
- Communication
- Conflict Management
- Customer Service
- Time Management
- Self Esteem

Hal's Most Requested Keynotes:
- 4 Secrets of Success. This reality-based keynote will motivate and inspire you to "take action" and realize your full potential and dreams. You will learn the "success secrets" that life's most successful people learned. They may not be what you think!
- 4 Secrets of Organizational Success. Learn what it takes to keep your organization successful and running smoothly. Discover the "success secrets" that the world's most successful organizations have discovered. They may not be what you think!

Clients Include:
- United States Army
- Toyota Corporation
- B.F. Goodrich
- American Pharmaceuticals
- Eden Industries
- Lane Community College
- GNB Technologies
- CGH Medical Center
- Plascom Corporation
- Waste Management
- OAG Corporation
- Heritage Newspaper
- Ernest Henry Mining
- Martin College
- Tumult Shire Council
- Statline
- Renoir Visions
- Woman's Hospital of Texas

What People Are Saying About Hal:

"With the problems I am currently having, I feel very motivated and excited to try the new techniques Hal taught today. It made me realize my errors and gave me ideas on how to do my job better."
—*Kristi Dexter, A/P Advisor*

"I think one of the best things about the training is that it gave me permission to excel as a manager. So often management is looked at as a necessary evil instead of the positive role that it is."
—*Natalie Brushar, Software Engineer Manager*

"Hal gave a very exciting as well as interesting workshop. There were times I needed to go to the bathroom but didn't because I was really into his training and didn't want to miss anything."
—*Eric Shoup, Supervisor*

"Hal did an excellent job. In my nine years as a nurse, this is the first seminar I've been to that held my total attention without getting drowsy throughout the program. My compliments."
—*Jannia East RN, Beaumant, Texas*

"Hal presented a great seminar. His enthusiasm is contagious."
—*Cynthia Kaelin, Licensing Coordinator, Little Rock, AK*

"This was the best seminar I've ever attended."
—*Steve Block, President, Hilliard Enterprises, Inc*

"Hal opened my eyes in many aspects of being a team leader. I would strongly recommend this workshop to anyone in a supervisory position."
—*Buddy Smith, Branch Manager, FNBank of Sharp County*

"I was dreading coming to this seminar today. Most are very boring. Hal kept my attention the whole time. He gave me information I can use."
—*Candice Kennedy. Manager, OK City*

"Best training our company has ever had! We'll have Hal back next year."
—*CGH Medical Center*

"Hal is an enthusiastic trainer. I usually fall asleep during seminars, but Hal kept me awake. —*Linda Beecher, Manager*

"I've been to lots of training, but Hal is by far the most energetic and dynamic trainer I've ever heard. And it takes a lot to make me happy."
—*Sue Grafton, Project Manager*

Also Available from *Power Potentials Publishing*

BOOK:

PowerPhrases®!
The Perfect Words to Say It Right and Get the Results You Want
by Meryl Runion

If you have ever walked away from a conversation because you didn't know what to say, or spoken in a way that backfired, *PowerPhrases!* is for you! If you have ever thought of the perfect thing to say AFTER it was too late, you need this book. This amazingly practical book addresses,

- What is a *PowerPhrase*?
- How to say "no" without caving in and losing friends
- What is a Killer Phrase?
- How to use *PowerPhrases* in conflict, sales, negotiations and work
- Create your own *PowerPhrases*
- Get conversations with strangers off to a quick and satisfying start
- Diffuse anger with *PowerPhrases*

   And much more.

A *PowerPhrase* is a short, specific expression that gets results by saying what you mean and meaning what you say without being mean when you say it. You will laugh with recognition as you see yourself in the "don't says" and sigh with understanding when you learn the most effective way to get your point across. *PowerPhrases* are what you should have said last time and will say next time

$21.95 – 210 pages ISBN #0-9714437-2-6

Also Available from *Power Potentials Publishing*

AUDIO:

PowerPhrases® for Rapid Resolution:
Conflict Management School *by Meryl Runion*

If coworkers, employees, bosses or even family members ever lead you to consider either becoming a hermit or homicide, you need solid conflict management tools to get through. Meryl provides the tools and a solid understanding of why conflict exists in the first place. What is the main cause of conflict? Conflicting needs? Differing perspectives? While these certainly contribute, the main cause of conflict is ineffective communication. This special audio provides you with the fundamental tools for managing conflict.

- Understand the difference between aggression and assertiveness.
- Take a revealing quiz to see where your conflict strengths and weaknesses are.
- Know the impact of your own thinking in conflict management.
- Learn the value of being concise.
- Discover the importance of being specific.
- Uncover what you really mean. Express your authentic position during conflict.
- Use strong emotions as a tool, not a weapon.
- Deal with disagreements without fanning the flames.
- Know the real message behind all those words.

Get the tools to stay calm in conflict, and the *PowerPhrases* to turn conflict into opportunity.

$21.95 — 2 Cassettes

Also Available from *Power Potentials Publishing*

AUDIO:

The Ten Secrets of Genuine Power *by Meryl Runion*

Are you powerful in the truest sense? Most people aren't! Meryl Runion of *Power Potentials* has made a study of power and shares her important but surprising discoveries in *The Ten Secrets of Genuine Power* Your first step in obtaining power is understanding what it is. Meryl provides this understanding with solid principles, concrete techniques and spellbinding stories. But she doesn't stop there. Meryl not only shows you what it means to be powerful, she gives you a step-by-step approach to unfold the amazing power already within you. In this inspiring and practical book you'll learn how to,

- Know exactly what you want.
- Put the inner voice of limitation in its proper place.
- Separate unfounded fears from genuine danger signs.
- Turn your thinking around 180°.
- Speak so you are respected AND liked.
- Uncover sources of power you never knew that you had.
  And much more.

$21.95 — 2 Cassettes

Also Available from *Power Potentials Publishing*

SPECIAL REPORT:

21 Secrets to Become a Treasured New Employee
by Meryl Runion

Are you new to the workforce? Or have you watched other, less talented employees pass you by with promotions while your potential goes unrecognized? This special report details the steps of becoming an indispensable at the workplace no matter what the economy is doing. This special report is essential for the new employee, valuable for the seasoned one.

Secrets include

- The 5 things every new employee needs to know to manage their boss.
- Quickly and easily understand and exceed employer expectations.
- Six secrets to getting anyone to like you – even strangers!
- Easily handle difficult people without becoming one.
- Build your support network using EOP–Enlightened Office Politics.
- You get what you ask for! – How to create an aura of dignity and respect.
- Broadcast basics – How to let 'em know you've got that winning attitude.
- The two fatal mistakes new employees make – and how to avoid them.
- Stand out while you fit in – how to represent your company and still be you.

This report gives you PRACTICAL action steps to excel at whatever you do, wherever you work.

$20.95 – Special report

Also Available from *Power Potentials Publishing*

SPECIAL REPORT:

Serve Your Customer Right:
PowerPhrases® for Customer Care
by Meryl Runion

Are you or your employees actually chasing away business unknowingly, by speaking in ways that alienate rather than attract customers? It costs five to six times more to find a new customer than to keep one you already have. Practical in nature, this special report tells you EXACTLY what to say and how to say it both every day and in your most challenging customer service scenarios to keep the customer coming back for more. Contents include,

- Turn complaint calls into opportunities.
- What to say to get customers to talk.
- Deal with difficult customers.
- Make someone's day.
- Get customer feedback.
- Create customer service oriented employees.
- What NOT to say in hundreds of customer service situations.

This is a Special Report that no business owner or manager should be without. It is filled not only with the best ways to get your message across to keep your customers, but common errors your employees are currently making that are costing you money.

$17.95 – Special Report

Free Newsletter from *Power Potentials*

A *PowerPhrase* a Week

Free weekly email newsletter telling of communication killers, the *PowerPhrase Principles* that were violated, and the most powerful ways to communicate in life situations you face every day. Develop your *PowerPhrases* savvy one week at a time.

Sign up today at *www.HowToSayIt.com*

Or email *PowerPhrases@att.net*

Privacy of emails is absolutely respected.

ORDER FORM

	Price	Quantity	Total
The Number One Secrets of Successful Managers *by Hal Pitt*	$21.95	x ____ =	_____
PowerPhrases!® The Perfect Words to Say it Right and Get the Results You Want *by Meryl Runion*	$21.95	x ____ =	_____
PowerPhrases® for Rapid Resolution: *by Meryl Runion*	$21.95	x ____ =	_____
The Ten Secrets of Genuine Power *by Meryl Runion*	$21.95	x ____ =	_____
21 Secrets to Become a Treasured New Employee *by Meryl Runion*	$20.95	x ____ =	_____
Serve Your Customer Right: **PowerPhrases® for Customer Care** *by Meryl Runion*	$17.95	x ____ =	_____

	SUBTOTAL:	_____
Colorado residents add 2.9% sales tax (multiply Subtotal by 0.029)	=	_____
Add $3.75 shipping for your first item $ 3.75		$ 3.75
Add $1.75 for each additional item $ 1.75	x ____ =	_____
	TOTAL:	_____

Send to: Power Potentials Publishing, P.O. Box 184, Cascade, CO 80809

Ship to:

Name _____

Address _____

City _____   State/Province _____   Zip/PC _____

Phone _____   *(We'll call if we have any problem with your order.)*

Enclose a check made payable to: *Power Potentials Publishing*

Thank you for your order

ORDER FORM

	Price	Quantity	Total
The Number One Secrets of Successful Managers *by Hal Pitt*	$21.95	x ___	= ___
PowerPhrases!® The Perfect Words to Say it Right and Get the Results You Want *by Meryl Runion*	$21.95	x ___	= ___
PowerPhrases® for Rapid Resolution: *by Meryl Runion*	$21.95	x ___	= ___
The Ten Secrets of Genuine Power *by Meryl Runion*	$21.95	x ___	= ___
21 Secrets to Become a Treasured New Employee *by Meryl Runion*	$20.95	x ___	= ___
Serve Your Customer Right: **PowerPhrases® for Customer Care** *by Meryl Runion*	$17.95	x ___	= ___

SUBTOTAL: ___

Colorado residents add 2.9% sales tax (multiply Subtotal by 0.029) = ___

Add $3.75 shipping for your first item $ 3.75 $ 3.75

Add $1.75 for each additional item $ 1.75   x ___   = ___

TOTAL: ___

Send to: Power Potentials Publishing, P.O. Box 184, Cascade, CO 80809

Ship to:

Name _____

Address _____

City _____ State/Province _____ Zip/PC _____

Phone _____ *(We'll call if we have any problem with your order.)*

Enclose a check made payable to: *Power Potentials Publishing*

Thank you for your order

ORDER FORM

	Price	Quantity	Total
The Number One Secrets of Successful Managers *by Hal Pitt*	$21.95	x ____ =	_____
PowerPhrases!® The Perfect Words to Say it Right and Get the Results You Want *by Meryl Runion*	$21.95	x ____ =	_____
PowerPhrases® for Rapid Resolution: *by Meryl Runion*	$21.95	x ____ =	_____
The Ten Secrets of Genuine Power *by Meryl Runion*	$21.95	x ____ =	_____
21 Secrets to Become a Treasured New Employee *by Meryl Runion*	$20.95	x ____ =	_____
Serve Your Customer Right: **PowerPhrases® for Customer Care** *by Meryl Runion*	$17.95	x ____ =	_____

		SUBTOTAL:	_____
Colorado residents add 2.9% sales tax (multiply Subtotal by 0.029)		=	_____
Add $3.75 shipping for your first item	$ 3.75		$ 3.75
Add $1.75 for each additional item	$ 1.75	x ____ =	_____
		TOTAL:	_____

Send to: Power Potentials Publishing, P.O. Box 184, Cascade, CO 80809

POWER POTENTIALS

Ship to:

Name

Address

City   State/Province   Zip/PC

Phone   *(We'll call if we have any problem with your order.)*

Enclose a check made payable to: *Power Potentials Publishing*

Thank you for your order